The Way and the Wilderness

The Way and the Wilderness

by

Kenneth Robinson

The Pentland Press Limited
Edinburgh · Cambridge · Durham
World Scientific Publishing Co., Inc., Singapore

First published in 1993 by
The Pentland Press Ltd.
1 Hutton Close
South Church
Bishop Auckland
Durham

With the co-operation of the World Scientific Publishing Company
of Singapore

ISBN 1 85821 083 6

Typeset by Elite Typesetting Techniques, Southampton.
Printed and bound by Antony Rowe Ltd., Chippenham.

Dedication

To the memory of Gwei-Djen
and her 'little sister'
Peggy
this book is affectionately
dedicated.

Introduction

Kenneth Robinson, my friend and collaborator since 1949, has written this book *The Way and the Wilderness.* It is, I believe, the kind of book which many people are looking for. If I may say so, I feel that it's just the kind of thing I might have written myself, when younger and more adventurously far-ranging. It poses the question – If you cannot accept the supernatural, yet are not insensitive to the numinous, what is the way forward? This book suggests that the philosophical Taoists of ancient China evolved a Way, the Tao, which may lead us out of our present wilderness. Kenneth Robinson suggests how their Way may be adapted to modern living.

Joseph Needham
Cambridge
8th October 1992.

'What is required is the formation in the minds of men of some kind of immunity mechanism against machinery, or rather against the peculiar mental bias associated with a life surrounded by machinery.'

Joseph Needham
The Great Amphibium, p.28.

'These are the days of miracle and wonder
This is the long distance call
The way the camera follows us in slo-mo
The way we look to us all
The way we look to a distant constellation
That's dying in a corner of the sky
These are the days of miracle and wonder
And don't cry baby, don't cry
Don't cry.'

Paul Simon
The Boy in the Bubble

'The world, if it has a future, has an ascetic future.'

Bruce Chatwin
The Songlines.

Contents

Foreword

Today we live in a time of change so rapid and so vast that it is difficult to keep events in any kind of perspective. For something comparable we must go back five hundred years to the fifteenth century when the old order was beginning to break down and people were compelled to rethink the most fundamental questions. At that time they had no idea what was causing their world to change. They were too close to the action. Was it that the Last Age was drawing nigh, to be followed by a stupendous bonfire? Was it that the Turks had been sent to punish Christians for their sins and follies? Or had it something to do with these new-fangled inventions of printing, gunpowder, and the magnetic compass?

Today we are more aware of changes, thanks to improvements in record keeping and the faster rate of change, but it is still difficult to discern the overall pattern of things. Are Europe and Asia, for example, a kind of giant seesaw, with China and Rome two thousand years ago in equilibrium, then Rome down and China up, then China down and Western Europe up, and now perhaps China and the Pacific rim countries coming up and Western Europe going down? Who knows? We also are too close to the action.

Five hundred years ago it was possible to believe that people ascended into Heaven, for everyone knew that the earth was flat, that Heaven was above, and Hell was below. The discovery of the Antipodes raised difficulties. Who goes up from down under? All such old time travellers would soon find themselves in orbit. But language comes to the rescue and metaphor leads like a kindly light those who have difficulty in changing their world image.

Because we are confronted by new questions to which there seem to be no clear answers our very sanity appears to be threatened. Is our world random or determined? If it is determined, who or what determined it? If it is random, why was it there in the first place? Why does it appear to be patterned, or is the patterning just one of our illusions? Are these perhaps just meaningless questions?

People who are worried by such questions sometimes turn to religion for reassurance. Our ancestral West-Eurasian religions have their roots in the Bronze Age. In those distant days priests and people alike believed in simple linear time. Everything began long ago, so it was said, and has been going on until now, and will continue till it comes to the end, and will then stop. 'And after that – what?' 'Eternity.' 'Eternal what?' Eternal adjectives and abstract nouns. Joyful. Damned. Bliss. Pain. Mercy. Love.

Einstein made it impossible to believe in linear time, though we may continue to use it for small-scale measurements between events, just as we continue to use Euclidean geometry for small-scale measurements of the earth's surface as if it were flat.

Nevertheless we continue to ask questions: Did everything that exists have a beginning, was it always there, or is the very idea of an ultimate beginning a crazy concept? If matter-energy had a beginning, was it created? Did it come about naturally? Or did it in fact not have a beginning? There is a large reading public which is avid for answers to these questions. But such metaphysical questions cannot be answered as yet. We must be content to recognise that people the world over fall into four groups – those who believe that there is a Creator who created everything from nothing; those who believe that what exists was not originally there, but somehow evolved naturally; those who believe that what exists was always there; and those who don't believe in any of these but are prepared to adopt one or other as a working hypothesis. The important thing is to treat those whose views differ from our own with the utmost courtesy and consideration.

This leads to another great question – moral behaviour. Morality varies in different societies. A society which is totally meek, far from inheriting the earth, may disappear from the face of it completely. The last few centuries are rich in examples of inoffensive peoples who have been eliminated. Meekness seems to need the backing of technological competence. The Bushmen of the Kalahari desert could perhaps have disseminated their kindness and courtesy to all the other populations of Southern Africa if they had had a higher level of technological competence at the outset. Now it is quite certain they will not inherit the earth.

But is technology also a snare? We have become aware of the dangers of putting our trust in 'reeking tube and iron shard'. But what of the gentler forms of compulsion? Lionel Elvin reminds me that human aggressivity which in the eighteenth century found an outlet in duelling was in the nineteenth century siphoned off into the lawcourts, just as in many lands lethal tribal conflicts were moderated into animated games of football or cricket or into boat races. Singapore has taken this process a stage further, and on the Metro has made it impossible for an aggressive person to fight his way on to a train, by controlling crowds with electronically operated doors. Those waiting to enter the train cannot be admitted until those leaving it are clear of the platform.Yet mechanisms can fail. The vital back-up is an intelligent understanding of the principles involved, reinforced by example. This brings us to the moral systems of the Chinese philosophers with which this book is partly concerned.

It is in the nature of human progress not to proceed in a straight line to an objective, but to tack – up-wind, down-wind – slowly closing on the desired end. There will doubtless be periods when society puts its main effort into constraining recalcitrant individuals by means of ingenious mechanisms and elaborate legislation into doing what it thinks is proper, and other times when society will react against laws and mechanisms for they can never cover all cases, and the example of saints and sages may seem more effective. Tacking is the order of the day – Confucian and Legalist pressure versus Taoist liberty and freedom of expression, *Yin* following *Yang* and *Yang* succeeding *Yin*. This approach to living is largely the subject matter of this book.

Above all it aims to help in some small degree the task of building bridges between different civilisations. This is perhaps the moment to acknowledge the part played by the people of two small islands – Singapore and Hongkong – in aiding the transfer of ideas in writing and in speech between East and West. Their bridge-building has been sustained by great generosity.

Part of our problem is to ensure that while year by year the transfer of ideas becomes technically simpler and quicker, the quality of ideas promoted, and the variety of products available, should not be reduced to suit the convenience of a machine-dominated civilisation.

Some readers of this book, meeting the word Taoism, may hope to find in it a mystical way out of the harsh realities of the world. That is hardly possible. The early philosophical Taoists appeal to me precisely because they were not mystical but came to grips with an extremely harsh and brutal world. They were adept at exploiting the resources of the subconscious mind, but that is a very different thing from being 'mystical' in the Western sense. They believed in the all-in-oneness of nature, in the totality of the universe in which the 'myriad things' are all interdependent and interacting, but not in a mystical 'One' to whom men pray, and who or which is above or beyond or in addition to the totality of nature. We are all aware that many things are at present inexplicable, but I do not find that a good reason for assuming that there is a supernatural element in nature.

People must decide what they wish to be. Either you are a supernaturalist or you are not. It is hard for supernaturalists to renounce the supernatural, for if they do so their warm and familiar world will appear to fall apart. How much, for example, of the Apostles' Creed remains if one cuts out the supernatural? Perhaps only 21 words. If Christianity were stripped of the supernatural what would be left? Perhaps just those things most essential to mankind's survival. Perhaps something not so very different from the principles of the early Taoist philosophers.

What does Taoism retain? It retains love in all its gradations, beginning with a small child fighting for its individuality and survival, but ending with the recognition of our insignificance in the immensity of the universe, made possible by the love of 'the myriad things', love broadened into a benign Buddhist-like compassion. Love makes possible all the other virtues most needed by human society – compassion, courage, self-sacrifice, generosity, non-aggressivity.

What else does Taoism offer? An awareness of the numinous in nature, that is to say, a feeling of reverence, wonder and awe at its immensity and complexity. What else? A desire to understand more fully how it all works, to realise we are part of the great cosmic dance, and to make some small contribution to the impetus of things, or as supernaturalists would say, to conform to the Divine Plan or Purpose. I would like to think that this book makes a small contribution to the impetus of things, but am aware that in reality it is no more than a pebble dropped into a pond. In writing it I have tried to express the problems and perplexities which face most of us ordinary people at the turn of the twentieth century. Answering problems is for the experts. 'Let the Hundred Schools contend'!

Let me now acknowledge the debt I owe to many people. When does a book start? Certainly long before the first words are written. My first acknowledgement must be to those who helped shape my thinking in the impressionable years, and especially my father who gave me the gift of doubt. When I was 26 I met Joseph Needham. Few young men who knew him in his prime could fail to be swept along by his dynamism, intellectual generosity, and originality of thought. He more than most taught me how to behave towards new ideas. He would go out to welcome a new idea, would warmly embrace it, turn it around lovingly in the light, and only if it was obviously flawed, if something obviously didn't ring true, would he reluctantly and sadly show it to the door and send it out into the night. Among others I would single out C.K. Ogden who brought home to me during World War Two that we were not fighting to keep pink spots on the map, a thought which was not so widely held before the fall of Singapore. Then there was Bernard Montgomery who warned: 'You must not get into battle on the wrong foot, gentlemen. You must not get into battle on the wrong foot!' But then the war itself was a great teacher, and a greater upsetter of fixed ideas. It brought me into contact with Neil Gokhale, maker of *The Tree of Life* and other films. So it has been with me, year by year, carried forward as on a river by the Tao, needing neither oar nor sail.

Coming finally to the book itself, I would like to thank most warmly those who read it in whole or in part at various stages when it was in draft, a time consuming task, especially when it comes to giving reasons for objections. Michael and Catherine Clark were helpfully critical of its early structure; Sylvia Haymon was meticulous for accuracy; Michael Shallis was the first of the scientists on whom I depended in writing Chapter 2. Kevin Kelly and my son James Robinson each carefully checked this same chapter at different stages in its evolution, and Professor Michael Kelly very kindly gave it a final reading. Professor

Lionel Elvin and his wife Margaret both read the finished text, and sent me several pages of detailed caution and encouragement. No less important to me were the general readers who gave me encouragement and telephone-time for discussion when we could not meet face to face. I am particularly grateful to Carolann Smith-Dorrien, John Moffett, John and Elspeth Pike and Simon and Audrey Cottrell for their enthusiasm and unstinted help.

It is a convention in lists such as this to put one's wife last. Really she should be first for a wife knows better than anyone how to make criticism acceptable. I have found the advice, criticism and encouragement given me by my Angela more precious than rubies.

1

The Spiritual Desert

The need for a way out of the spiritual wilderness of modern life was recognised as long ago as 1931 when Joseph Needham described in his book *The Great Amphibium* how machinery was driving us 'ever further forward towards the domination of the quantitative and the collapse of religious feeling'. An indicator of the influence of machinery on our thinking is to be found in the way newspapers are often packed with statistical trivia. '22,345 bathers made use of the city swimming bath between 12 p.m. last Monday and this morning, it is computed'!

The Industrial Revolution inevitably encouraged precise measurement and statistics. Some may now wish to put the clock back to an idyllic rural age. 'But,' Needham continued, 'nothing can come of a mere backward movement. Technological unemployment, which has caused so much machine-wrecking in the past, has really nothing to do with machines as such.' We cannot hope to get back to a golden age without machines. Without machines half the world's population would starve. 'What is required is the formation in the minds of men of some kind of immunity mechanism against machinery, or rather against the peculiar mental bias associated with a life surrounded by machinery.' Western civilisation has held the centre of the stage for some three hundred years. Now after two world wars and a groping after economic theory which is closer to alchemy than science, it shows signs of disintegration and moral collapse. When one civilisation begins to fail it is wise to study others. In an ancient book called *Yueh Ling* (Monthly Ordinances) the Chinese described what may well serve as a model or prototype for the sort of mechanism we are now looking for. It may be that in the long history of China with its golden thread of Taoism and its emphasis on holism, Western civilisation can find a way to heal itself, can find a way out of the wilderness. So let us now consider deserts.

Today the whole world is under threat of becoming a desert. Some survivors there might certainly be, but perhaps not many. Few can live in a desert. It is a cruel, beautiful and interesting place. It is always changing. There are shifts of light as the sun moves across the sky, and if it is hilly, the architecture is altered by the wind.

A desert has strict rules for the creatures that live in it. The rules of the desert formed the framework for the religions which sprang up within the Fertile Crescent. The sharp dividing line between the desert and the sown is ideal for legislators who like clear distinctions and hate blurred edges. Naturally the gods of the Fertile Crescent were great legislators. The Peoples of the Book learnt to read between well-ruled lines.

From time to time rain falls in the desert making it 'bloom like the rose', or at least giving some indication of its potential. The desert is not utterly without mercy. It grants an occasional reprieve.

An urban desert is a very different matter. It is full of noise, never ceasing, like the pounding of the Pacific on the Great Barrier Reef, but less melodious. Its architecture is sculpted by decay. When the wind blows across it, heaven's breath is tangy with chemicals. The creatures that live in it obey strict rules, some of them imposed from above, and some of their own devising. The two sets are often contradictory. Any person who is obliged to obey both sets of rules simultaneously needs to be quick-thinking and sure-footed.

A spiritual desert differs yet again. Ancient rules have broken down, and new ones have not yet been formulated. This desert is a grey expanse, ill-defined and trackless, with people wandering about in the half-light, looking after themselves as best they can, gathering sour berries from endless thorny bushes. No-one bothers to look up, for no stars are visible in the murk overhead. No chance to get one's direction. All that can be done is to keep one's eyes on the bushes, and try to get more sour berries than anyone else.

The grey desert of the thorn bushes, and the desert of creeping decay are often the same place. One is within and the other is without. You may look at the droves of people with their heads down following the grey pavement, as they press forward to some place where the berries grow more profusely. No time to stop! Yet occasionally one of them will draw aside, look up at the sky to see if it is clearing a little, or stand listening intently to the roar all about him. He thinks he can hear lake water lapping with low sounds by the shore.

Dismal though the scene may be, we should not complain. There is a certain rough justice in events. The Way of Nature, the Tao as it is called in China, is not mocked. If for a time the pendulum swings excessively to one side, it is certain to be followed in due course by an excessive swing to the other, action and reaction being equal and opposite. The way of the Sage is to moderate the excesses and achieve a working harmony.

If the way of the Sage is not followed, birds will later come home to roost. For example, is it unjust that Britain should now be subjected to drugs flooding in from the 'golden triangle', seeing that less than a century and a half ago we were using our naval power to make it impossible for Lin Tê-hsü and other good but other hard-pressed Governors of the provinces of a

China riddled with corruption to prevent our opium from entering their country? How right that Britain, which grew rich by exporting slaves, should in turn make a home for their descendants as the pendulum swings back. Is it surprising that the Church, which for so many centuries intimidated its congregations with threats of hell-fire, should now, in the twentieth century, find people who have lost their fear of hell-fire looting of their unguarded treasures churches which for centuries had never locked their doors? This pendulum of events, this Yin-Yang rhythm, is not to be ignored. The Tao is not mocked.

As this book develops we shall gradually come to terms with Taoist expressions and ways of thought, but perhaps now is the moment to make a start. The word *Tao* itself, from which the word Taoism is formed, is now spelt *Dao* in China, since this is held to be nearer to the sound as spoken in Chinese, rhyming with the English words 'how' and 'now'. *Tao* means a road or path, and more generally a way, and the way in which things happen or a way of doing things. So it also came to mean the way of Nature, the way of the universe, how the whole thing works.

In ancient China, and in ancient India[1], it was assumed not that a Creator had created everything, but either that the stuff of the universe had always been there, or that it had evolved from nothing. Modern science has advanced this thinking a little by suggesting that what is not actually there may nevertheless be there as a potential. In India the possibilities were debated in the seventh or even eighth centuries before our era in the *Chandogya Upanisad* as to whether being could come from non-being. In China thinkers were convinced that the Tao was a permanence.

Thinking about the Tao, its immensity and its complexity, could not but induce a feeling of awe. One does not joke about Black Holes, nor, for all the flippancy of the term, is the Big Bang a laughing matter. The explanations given by Chinese thinkers of the third century about how the world began are not of course to be regarded as scientific in the modern sense, but as enquiries on rationalist lines into how the universe could have begun. Because the enquiries were rational Taoist thinking can without difficulty be updated.

There are perhaps three other terms which occur frequently in Taoist books, which need to be seen in modern perspective. These are: *ch'i*, now spelt *qi*; *yin-yang* and *wu-wei*.

There is a tendency in modern books which promote mysticism to give these terms a validity which they don't deserve, as if they enshrined some inner wisdom or truth. Let us look into them in detail. The word *ch'i* is a primitive notion which over the centuries gradually became more sophisticated. Originally it meant steam arising from the cooking pot, and by extension many other sorts of vapour. Later it was thought of as a sort of celestial breath which, when cold and condensed, becomes heavy matter like metal or stone, and when hot and rarified becomes light and gaseous like flame. It may be compared with ancient Greek ideas of *pneuma* or spiritual breath – holy spirit. There is no obvious justification at present for using such terms except in a poetical or historical context.

The next term for closer inspection is *yin-yang*, or the *yin* and the *yang*. This term is gradually making itself at home in the English language, and with more reason, but nevertheless must be used with discrimination. *Yang* originally meant the sunny side of a hill, and *yin* meant the shady side of a hill. It would have been immediately acceptable to the farmers of Celtic Britain who traditionally grew corn on their *yang* fields and pastured cattle on their *yin* fields. However, the terms *yin* and *yang* soon expanded to cover all sorts of related ideas. The *yang* was not only sunny and warm and bright, but represented all those qualities which a male-dominated society likes to attribute to the male sex – vigour, growth, aggressivity, masculinity, openness and so on, whereas the *yin* was thought of as feminine, yielding, secretive, cool, dark and passive. All over the world one finds contrasting lists of qualities, often with the good qualities attributed to the male and the bad qualities attributed to the female. But China's contribution in formulating the *yin-yang* concept was to stress that light and dark, male and female, and so on are not, as the ancient Persians believed, competitive but *complementary*. The sexes are complementary, not hostile. The *yin* and the *yang* follow each other in rhythmic succession. There is no ultimate victory for either, but a natural ebb and flow.

We shall speak later on of how the Chinese used the *yin-yang* concept to express certain mathematical ideas, but *yin-yang* as a scientific term has long been superseded. It may, however, still legitimately be used as a poetic expression to suggest the ebb and flow of events, the tides in the affairs of men. The affairs of men are usually of such complexity as to defy scientific analysis. When we see the term *yin-yang* on a printed page it may therefore be taken as a signal that we are talking poetically and not scientifically. Poetic writing can be no less instructive and inspiring than scientific writing – sometimes more so. But it is important to be clear in one's mind in which mode language is being used.

Finally there is the term *wu-wei* which means 'not interfering with the processes of nature'. This does not mean doing nothing at all. More positively it means 'using or taking advantage of the natural flow of events'. This idea lies at the heart of Taoist behaviour, and particularly affects our attitude to the environment. Much will be said about it later on. Meanwhile let us now return to the *Yin* and the *Yang*, and assimilate them into our vocabulary.

The Yang – that which is hot, bright and strong, will, in the fullness of time, give way to the Yin, to that which is cool, dark and yielding. Captured nations in the end capture their conquerors. When the Yang is at its zenith it is difficult to believe that it holds within itself the seeds of decay. In 1940 Germany, with the hot bright strength of martial youth, seemed invincible. And when, two and a half thousand years earlier, the Jews had been led into captivity in Babylon, how could they foresee any way of escape or deliverance? But things have their seasons. Times change. In the dark hour, deep in the recesses of our minds, we must cultivate the glimmering pearl, which is a vision of a Yin world that functions not as a result of force but out of consideration for others. That means a world where, even if one has suffered injustice, one feels no resentment. The Tao will correct injustices in its own time. 'Vengeance is mine,' saith the Lord. 'I will repay.'

To change the moral basis of society is a long-term business. The police are therefore likely to be with us for centuries. In the years to come the common people may well think back with nostalgia to the days of our sturdy ancestors who declared they would rather be murdered in their beds than have a police force. The grip of the police will tighten. Already the word of one honest man in a court of law is worth less than the word of two bent policemen, because the man is not known to be honest, and the policemen are not known to be bent. Even worse, the word of one honest man is worth less than that of a wrongly-fed computer. Machines are thought to be more truthful than human beings. The basis of our future morality is therefore likely to be computer-led. And if by chance, or error, or malevolence, false information about a man is fed to a computer to which the authorities have access, he may never know what is holding him back in his career, and if he does find out, he can spend the rest of his life in fruitless efforts to obtain justice. But let it never be forgotten that this state of affairs is not permanent.

Today the most influential members of Western society find themselves from birth heirs to a gross and often obscene materialism. But the pleasure of possessions tends to pall. Refinement of taste demands always something more exquisite; there is no end to acquisition, no ultimate happiness that way. The entrepreneur who pulls down his warehouses to build greater, may not find that his soul is immediately required of him, but after a time a certain weariness sets in and an emptiness follows him into retirement. Ripples of weariness spread through society, even to those who have never had it so good. Some feel revulsion, some apathy, and a large proportion of society is alienated. Nostalgically we in Britain think back to times when things were different, to some idealised Elizabethan Age. No earlier age was ever ideal, but previous generations in almost all walks of life felt they belonged. Why should things today be so different? What is it that has hit us?

What has hit us is something like a tidal wave following a nuclear explosion. The explosion was an intellectual and social explosion that began about five centuries ago, and is still going on. Before it took place the world was fairly stable. In the West there was Christendom, a loose assemblage of princes, who nevertheless had a good deal in common in their ideas about life, religion, the beginning of the world, death, war and the Latin language.

In the East there was China, both stable and dynamic, held together by Confucianism, wealthy, not often aggressive, self-centred and becoming rather self-satisfied. In Central Asia, however, was something resembling a rather unpredictable volcano. Periods of quiescence would be followed by periods of furious activity in which waves of nomadic people were suddenly set in motion, and spilled over the frontiers of the surrounding kingdoms. These were the Scyths, Huns, Mongols, Turks and many others, attacking the empires of India, Persia, Parthia and Egypt, as well as the walled empires of China and Rome. This had been going on for centuries, but about the time that William the Conqueror was preparing to invade England, a change occurred. This was that the earlier Chinese invention of gunpowder was now followed in that country by the development of bombs and rockets of considerable sophistication, and then by cannon, an invention which made its way across Asia with surprising speed.

The Chinese invented gunpowder and cannon, but didn't fully exploit their invention. This was not because the Chinese were an unwarlike people. Far from it. It was partly because their saltpetre fields were overrun by the barbarians, and scarcity of nitrates crippled experiment. Partly also they lacked targets comparable to the fortresses of European feudal nobles. Early cannon were best used against fortifications, but China's enemies, being nomads, didn't lock themselves up in fortresses. How Chinese bombards and cannon made their way to the West is a complex story. The use which was made of them in the West is already too well known. The walls of Constantinople were breached in the year 1453 by a gigantic gun made for the Turkish sultan by a Hungarian engineer. Feudal castles were battered down, and powerful centralised nation states ruled by artillery-owning kings became the new order of Europe. By the time of Napoleon the gun had become 'the queen of the battlefield', and ships had been built so sturdy and large that they could deliver a ripple-fire discharge of shot 'broadside'. But this awakening to the possibilities of chemistry was only one aspect of the growing technological and intellectual explosion in Europe.

Far more frightening was the collapse of the Aristotelian universe. This had been a universe of great stability. Change was believed to occur only near its centre, the Earth. The moon circled the Earth, and all below it was known as the sublunary sphere. Beyond the sublunary sphere all was perfect and unchanging, moving forever in perfect circles. God had given it this perfection. To doubt it was to doubt the omnipotence of God. This stable universe collapsed on the evening of November 11th 1572, when the Danish astronomer Tycho Brahe observed a new star blazing furiously in the remote region of the fixed stars where God had arranged that nothing ever changes, and where certainly no new star ought to be.

Admittedly there had been misgivings about the heavens before, but it had not been possible to disprove the theory of the great Aristotle, which had been assimilated into Christian belief. When Tycho Brahe saw it, he had to be very careful. Perhaps it wasn't a new star at all. Perhaps his eyes deceived him. Perhaps it was an unusual meteorite. But other people saw it, and Tycho Brahe had the most accurate astronomical instruments in the world at that time. He found that it didn't move, and that it was new, that there had in fact been a change in the sphere of the outermost fixed stars. What occurred in November 1572 was the explosion of a *supernova.*

Five years later, in 1577, a comet arrived. These had always been regarded as sublunary, as transient creatures perfectly entitled to exist in the sphere just above the Earth where change is known to take place. But Tycho Brahe, with the new capacity of his instruments for accurate measurement, was able to show that it was many times farther out into space than the moon. The old order was breaking down. Heresies grew apace, as that the universe was infinite and peopled with innumerable worlds not unlike our own. This came from the ravings of the ex-Dominican friar magician Giordano Bruno. In 1600 he was very properly burnt alive as an act of 'clemency' on the Campo di Fiori in Rome after five years in prison and two of interrogation by the Inquisition, in vain.

Worse was to come. It had previously been believed that the universe had been made by God, and that there was a reason for everything which He had made. Why then had He made the myriads of stars? Clearly, to adorn the sky for Man's pleasure, who, seeing them in their beauty would give Him praise. But in the year 1609 Galileo, learning about the new 'optick tubes', constructed the first genuine astronomical telescope[2] capable of magnifying what was seen nine times. The result – stars which had never been seen before in the history of man leapt into view! If God had really made the stars for Man's pleasure, why had He been keeping them out of sight all this time? Vexing questions began to multiply. Sir Walter Raleigh had crossed the Atlantic and started a colony in Virginia. He knew a thing or two about little ships and how much they could carry. When he came to write his *History of the World* he could not but be sceptical as to whether Noah could really have got a pair of animals of every surviving species, together with the fodder needed for them, and food for his own family, into a small ship made of gopher wood, so that they could remain afloat for 150 days before starting to recolonise a drowned world. All over Europe men and women started asking difficult questions.

There were, for example, many more different types of animal than Noah had ever dreamed of. Explorers in South America saw for the first time llamas and armadilloes, and later, at the other side of the Pacific, the duck-billed platypus, the dodo, the emu and the booby. Plants, insects and fish were also observed in unbelievable profusion, and specimens were brought back to Europe. How could they be classified? They frequently did not seem to belong to Aristotle's categories. The whole method of thinking had to be altered. The methods of the merchant were introduced to help in this world-wide stocktaking. How much did things measure? How much did they weigh? How best could they be classified so that you could find them when you wanted them? What could you do with them? How did they work? In what way were they different from the things already known? How could they be tested to make sure? Questions such as these gradually led the early scientists, the natural philosophers, to develop the 'scientific method'.

Another element in the explosion was the building of the great ships which could cross the oceans and reach distant lands. They sailed, guided by a Chinese invention, the magnetic compass, and armed with up to 110 heavy guns. Not far behind the guns were the servants of the Lord God of Hosts, the missionaries. Just as once the nomadic tribes had streamed across the plains of Central Asia to overwhelm the kingdoms and empires which they found in their way, so now the Europeans, just emerging from barbarism, destroyed or assimilated the peoples and empires which they found in their path, when they had crossed the oceans. There followed the heyday of Catholic expansion in the years when Spain, Portugal and France were the leading powers, resulting in permanent mass conversions in South America, and less successful attempts at conversion of the long established and sophisticated peoples of the East.

Of particular interest was the Jesuit mission to China, which began its fruitful work in the year 1580. Knowledge flowed both ways – into China about Western mathematics, astronomy and many other subjects; out of China and back to Europe about botany, zoology, music, theory of government, and many other stimulating matters which fed the European intellectual explosion. Like the Greeks on the plains of Troy the Jesuit Fathers went bearing gifts. They used the newly invented striking clocks and scientific instruments as their wooden horse with which to breach the walls of the Chinese citadel. The Chinese were pleased with the clocks, amused by the Western barbarians' curious theories about the heavenly bodies encircling the earth on crystalline spheres, and quite unconvinced by the theology which was said to be the basis for these theories.[3] Then the Jesuit Fathers began to receive more than they gave. Their activities had, by the beginning of the eighteenth century, come to be regarded as a threat to Christianity itself, and after a period of violent controversy marked by papal bulls and decrees, a brief suppressing the Society in China was promulgated in the year 1773.

There followed an uneasy period during which Europe was experiencing such events as the breakaway of the American colonies to become the United States, the French Revolution, the conquest of India, the Industrial Revolution, the wars against Napoleon and the rush for colonies. The Protestant countries were now extremely active, and the rest of the world had to submit to the ministrations of their missionaries. In China the age of discussion between equals was over. The new wave of missionaries was not only backed by the military might of their governments, but with the compelling arguments of the new science. Eager to spread the latest ideas on hygiene and public health, Western administrators, doctors and missionaries succeeded in cutting back the death rates in countries where they found themselves. They did little about cutting back the birth rates also, with the result that these countries today have acquired huge populations which can scarcely be fed, and whose increase can only be restrained by fierce legislation.

This was the great age of optimism and confidence. Never was confidence so insecurely based! Science was advancing with giant strides. Geology was establishing the age of the Earth. The Bible story of the creation of the world was coming to be seen as Babylonian legend. The theory of evolution was formulated, with Man on his way up and up. Mathematics was solving problem after problem. Kant in 1755 proposed that the world had evolved as part of one of the newly observed spiral whorls in space, as part of a galaxy. Laplace developed his fully determinist theory of the universe, and when asked by Napoleon about the role of God in his *System of the World*, is said to have replied, not irreverently, that he had no need of that hypothesis. The Garden of Eden was forever lost.

But in some parts of the world the conception lingered on of the earth floating above the waters of the deep, and protected against the waters outside by the dish cover of the sky. All this had been created by the Great Architect of the Universe. In mid-September 1959, however, I was in a Dayak longhouse in Sarawak. The radio announced that the Russian space probe *Luna II* had crashed on to the surface of the moon. Although the Americans at first described it as nothing more than 'a hunk of old iron', the Dayaks in whose house I was staying declared that it was impossible for it to have landed on the moon at all. Why? Because, if it had, it would have made a hole through the sky, and if there was a hole in the sky the water would come through, and we should be having terrible rain; no doubt the sort of rain that Noah had had to put up with. The 14th September 1959 may perhaps be taken as the date on which this view of the universe finally became untenable.

It had already gone in Europe by the time of the battle of Waterloo. The mathematics of Newton had given a new universe a seemingly unshakeable stability, with foundations set so fast that it seemed they never could be moved. Isaac Newton died in the year 1727. In his lifetime he had announced the fundamental laws of dynamics and the laws of universal gravity. He was not the first person to notice that an apple falls to the ground, but he was the first to show that gravity is a universal force. After his death the world men knew was no longer the same. The universe seemed to be full of orbs all spinning like wheels with the regularity of clockwork. But just like eighteenth century clocks, their regularity was not perfect. There were small irregularities in the behaviour of the planets, of meteorites, comets and so on, which suggested that God, who made this sublime piece of clockwork mechanism, had to be present all the while adjusting it and keeping it wound up. God had become a clockmaker and clockminder.

A century later, however, astronomy and mathematics had both made great advances, and it was felt that most of the irregularities which had disturbed Newton did not exist, but were to be attributed to faulty observation, or to miscalculation in mathematics, or would be corrected by self-regulating mechanisms. God came, therefore, to be regarded as the originator of the universe, as the author of the laws of nature, and as a benign spectator of events. The perfect author of a perfect creation cannot alter it. It would be illogical to suggest that there was any need for tampering. Yet in its turn Newton's universe was also undermined despite its apparent strength.

Newton made possible the full-blown determinism of the nineteenth century. Everything proceeded according to mechanical laws. Everything was in theory predictable. If men could not predict many things very far ahead, this was merely because the complexities were too much for their inadequate brains. But for an omniscient God there were no problems. In the full pride of their confidence in the omniscient God whose plan they were carrying out, the missionaries moved in on those countries whose lack of modern science left them vulnerable, searching for souls to save from damnation.

In heathen lands afar
Thick darkness broodeth yet.
Arise, O morning star,
Arise and never set.

But even while they were contemplating the morning star, it began to be obscured by an unfortunate fog arising in the homeland of this comfortable doctrine. If God was infinite, unchanging and everlasting, he could not logically limit his action to a small part of time and space. Nor was it logical to imagine an infinite universe existing only for a limited duration. An infinite and eternal world that has been created is a contradiction. It does not need creation. There is no need of this hypothesis. 'It exists by virtue of its very infinity.'[4] Inexorably the Europeans were moving in the direction of a Taoist view of life.

As Alexandre Koyré has said, 'The Divine Artifex had therefore less and less to do in the world. He did not even need to conserve it, as the world, more and more, became able to dispense with this service.' By the end of the nineteenth century there was an infinite universe moving endlessly and aimlessly in eternal space, following eternal and necessary laws. In this determinist universe there was no scope for free will, and little sense of purpose or inspiration. At this point mankind began to enter the wasteland. The Industrial Revolution which, two hundred years before, had been only a smudge of black smoke and a dirty stream in a green valley, blossomed out into gaunt cities of endless rows of terrace houses, richly endowed with smog, from which all wild life had fled except the persistent rat and the audacious sparrow. It was at this point that many people gave up trying to make sense of the universe, and would fall back on some such phrase as 'It's all a great mystery'. Meanwhile the power which the Industrial Revolution had unleashed found sinister outlets. The days when armies went to war supported by such supplies of food and ammunition as could be dragged to the firing lines by horses pulling carts, were drawing to a close. First railways were pressed into the service of war, bringing far greater quantities of ammunition to the soldiers than they had ever had before, dumping it at railhead, and leaving it to be brought forward by short hauls in carts and waggons. Then lorries were invented, distribution of ammunition was enormously improved, and such glamour as the battlefield might once have had, disappeared in the Flanders mud.

Before the next war was ready to break out there had been a rush of new inventions. The speed with which they arrived was breathtaking. Humanity needs at least a generation to assimilate a new idea, otherwise the generation gap occurs in which the old people cannot understand what their children are talking about. In my father's lifetime, and before I was born, gas balloons had been followed by fairly efficient kites and gliders, which then became motorised and air travel had begun. In 1938 I met an old man, appropriately named Mr Bird, who, in 1892, as a boy of twelve, had sat on a plane driven by steam, and flown across a field and over a hedge.[5] Within his generation and mine flight has advanced from a hop across a hedge to a landing on the moon.

Along with increasing speed in travel came increasing ease and speed in communication, in computerised calculation, in mechanised and then automated production, and in the proliferation of research. The demand for scientists doubles every ten or fifteen years. No nation can meet such demands. It therefore becomes necessary for scientists to be directed or attracted into high priority areas. Naturally, the high priority areas are war-making, euphemistically called 'defence', and industry, particularly those industries which feed defence. Unless these priorities are altered, the more benign areas of science will become progressively starved of resources. But by what complex process are these priorities decided?

The age of confident optimism was coming to an end by the start of the present century. This was neatly expressed in verse:

> Nature and Nature's law lay hid in night;
> God said, 'Let Newton be!' and all was light.
> It didn't last; the Devil howling 'Ho!
> Let Einstein be!' restored the status quo.[6]

Einstein used to refer to God as 'The old One'. He always kept a place for him in his heart, but it was as if the role of the deity had been reduced from Architect to Clockmaker to Clock-minder to Old Age Pensioner. Einstein performed the remarkable feat of ushering in the new age with his eyes in wistful gaze upon the past. He was the hinge between the old and the new. But it was he who for the first time related Time indissolubly to Space.

Children have little sense of time because they haven't seen much change, and what changes they have seen seem to take place very slowly. But as we get older the impression of change builds up, time begins to hasten, then to gallop and finally to race past. It can only be delayed by abstracting the mind from its obsession with transient phenomena. The more time is speeded up, the more transient these phenomena appear. It is only during the twentieth century that we have begun to get some control over time. By the use of time-lapse photography we are able to see the dandelion swaying like a ballet dancer in its death struggle with the dodder plant as the two writhe and twist together in their rooted pursuit and flight, until the dandelion is lassoed and held in deadly embrace. The hunting and grappling which was meaningless to us when extended over a period of weeks, assumes form when it is speeded up by cinematography and projected in a matter of minutes.

The same can be done for slower processes. The bare branches of an oak tree can be made to sprout, put out pale leaves, be smothered in the dark green of summer, turn yellow, then brown and finally stand naked once again under wintry skies all in a matter of minutes. But the life of the oak tree itself is beyond the range of any single man. To see illusion on the grand scale one must resort to imagination. In his novel *The Time Machine* H.G Wells did just that. His Time Traveller had built a machine capable of travelling along a time 'dimension' – something which Wells later confessed was an author's sleight of hand. The Time Traveller sat on his machine, and after a few short trial runs, pulled the lever hard over and flung himself into the future.

'The night came like the turning out of a lamp, and in another moment came tomorrow. The laboratory grew faint and hazy, then fainter and ever fainter. Tomorrow night came black, then day again, night again, day again, faster and faster still . . . As I put on pace, night followed day like the flapping of a black wing. The dim suggestion of the laboratory seemed presently to fall away from me, and I saw the sun hopping swiftly across the sky, leaping it every minute, and every minute marking a day. I supposed the laboratory had been destroyed and I had come into the open air . . . Then, in the intermittent darkness, I saw the moon spinning swiftly through her quarters, from new to full, and had a faint glimpse of the circling stars. Presently, as I went on, still gaining velocity, the palpitation of night and day merged into one continuous greyness; the sky took on a wonderful deepness of blue, a splendid luminous colour like that of early twilight; the jerking sun became a streak of fire, a brilliant arch, in space; the moon a fainter fluctuating band; and I could see nothing of the stars, save now and then a brighter circle flickering in the blue . . . I saw huge buildings rise up faint and fair, and pass like dreams. The whole surface of the earth seemed changed – melting and flowing under my eyes . . . And so my mind came round to the business of stopping . . . But to come to a stop . . . meant bringing my atoms into such intimate contact with those of the obstacle that a profound chemical reaction – possibly a far-reaching explosion – would result[7] . . .

This story was published in 1895, when Einstein was sixteen, and ten years before the publication of his 'Special Theory of Relativity'. In 1895 atoms were still an assumption. Their existence had not yet been proved. But by 1895 the smell of relativity was already in the air, and in that very year Wilhelm Roentgen discovered X-rays. In the following year Henri Becquerel discovered radioactivity, and in 1898 the Curies isolated radium, the year after Thomson had discovered the carrier of electricity – the 'corpuscule' known as the electron.

From this time forward the world which had been established during the previous centuries began to collapse, and the human race was swept into the future on the racing current of nuclear discoveries. One current was fed by Einstein's theory of relativity; the other was the new quantum theory which was hammered into shape by a number of different minds and personalities. Until the year 1900 mankind lived in a solid-seeming world extending outwards through several different levels of organisation to the most distant stars, but securely based on molecules which organised themselves as matter which resisted his touch, reflected colours to his eyes, vibrated in ripples of sound to his ears, passed information about their constituents to his tongue as taste, and drifted into his nostrils with similar information interpreted as smell. Everything in this world could be pictured or reduced to something like pictorial symbols. Although men could not see molecules when they first began to think about them, they could be visualised as very small things like sparks or motes of dust, but much smaller. When they thought of atoms, they imagined these very small things broken up into yet smaller pieces, until finally they reached what could no longer be divided, the atom or unsplittable.

After 1900 'the whole surface of the earth seemed changed'. What tottered the edifice of traditional physics was the shock of two discoveries, the electron and radioactive disintegration. It was now evident that at least some of the 'atoms', so far from being inert and passive fragments of matter, mere building blocks of the universe, were themselves in a state of high activity.

For a time the educated public were able to follow developments in the world of physics. Roentgen's X-rays immediately fired public imagination, partly because of his seemingly macabre photographs of the human skeleton, partly because of the possibilities they appeared to open up. *Punch* for example published a humorous illustration with the caption: 'Using the new X-rays Herr Roentgen takes a photograph of his bedroom door!' This showed an ordinary bedroom door, and crouching behind it his landlady peering through the keyhole.

Einstein's theory of relativity, though to the general public the last word in bafflement, nevertheless came to be assimilated in large measure as the concept of the space-time continuum, in contrast to the earlier notions of space and time having dimensions. When jokes circulate about scientific discoveries it is an indication that they are having an impact on public consciousness. The theory of relativity may be said to have had an impact on public consciousness when people began to repeat the limerick:

There was a young lady from Wight
Who could travel faster than light.
She set off one day
In a relative way
And returned on the previous night.

But quantum theory was another matter. Physicists were now talking about things which could no longer be pictured, in which words appeared to be used in contradictory senses, in which new terms were being freely invented as labels for things which could not be imagined, which depended for their understanding on mathematics far beyond the capacity of the man in the street, and in which the conclusions arrived at appeared to be utter paradoxes. A great gulf began to open up between the ordinary man and the specialists, such as the world had not seen since the priests of Ancient Egypt distanced themselves from the common man by the interposition of high level mysteries. Perhaps it was greater even than that, for the Egyptian priests were specialists at the higher levels of a religious idea shared with the common man, whereas the world concept derived from the ideas of Copernicus, Kepler and Newton had little in common with that held by the people who still believed that the earth was flat. A similar qualitative difference exists between the Newtonian universe which is still the background for the thinking of most educated people today, and that of quantum physics.

The twentieth century became the age of quantum physics. Quantum theory was something which Einstein was never able wholly to accept. And that is not surprising, for in its early years it seemed to reintroduce the ancient nightmare of the Greeks – a chaotic universe. Empedocles had said that creation once started was a matter of chance, and Democritus believed that the atoms of which his world was composed had no beginning and no end, but were swept along at random, colliding from time to time to form complex substances. This was heady stuff, made tolerable to some by the idea of Love binding together, while Hate drives apart – a primitive formulation of the concepts of attraction and repulsion. But Greek intellectual daring did not long survive the death of their democracies. The comforting Logos, the intelligible pattern of the universe, which their contemporaries in China would have found to be a perfectly acceptable idea, became exalted into a supreme principle, 'in the beginning was the Word', and in Christian times was identified with Jesus Christ. From then on Western Europe was in the hands of the Eternal Father, strong to save. This lasted until Newton ushered in the age of determinism, which itself began to break down at the beginning of the twentieth century.

Now we find ourselves like the Ionian Greeks trying to grapple with a completely new world, or rather, with an unexpected and astonishing universe. At the level at which we are accustomed to think, there are molecules, aggregations of stable stuff. These combine to form bodies which we recognise through our senses. They can be seen, touched, tasted, and so on. Such aggregations form bodies of different sizes. At one end of the scale they are so small that they can only be seen with microscopes. At the other end they are so large and yet so distant that they can only be seen with telescopes. These bodies are organised in degrees of complexity, from the utterly simple to the extremely complex. In our own bodies many molecules are organised to make a cell, and millions of cells make up a person's body. At a vaster level, the body on which we live, the Earth, together with its companion bodies, moons, satellites, planets, stellar debris, dust and gas, forms part of an organisation centred on the sun. This is the solar system. At a vaster level still our own solar system is organised along with the millions of other systems in the swirl of light which we call the Milky Way. At this level we are dealing with galaxies. All the galaxies which can be detected are assumed to form a system which may be called the Universe. We are not yet in a position to know whether other universes form yet vaster systems beyond our range. However, the possibility that 'our universe is indeed just one bubble among many in some greater meta-universe' is now seriously considered.[8]

At the level of the molecule sensation is possible. There is something to push against. At the level of the atom it is possible no longer. That this would probably be so was understood some twenty-four centuries ago in fourth century Athens. The Democritean school believed that atoms were the result of a division carried to the last possible stage, the residue of 'unsplittables'.

These atoms underwent no changes experienced by our senses. They were neither wet nor dry, gave forth no smell, were colourless, tasteless, and without temperature. They varied, however, in size and shape, and possessed the power of motion. They moved in empty spaces. Epicurus elaborated the theory a little further by saying that they also had weight. Being changeless they were eternal. Change consisted in the ways in which they were grouped, the patterns they made in the ceaseless dance of the universe.

Rather than accept that the world and its universe is a chaotic jungle in which everything is for ever changing, the Greeks speculated that in unchanging atoms there might be a solid basis for everything, and that if the atoms made patterns, there was reason for believing that there was order in the universe. If there was order in the universe, then it should be possible eventually to predict what was likely to happen next. This was speculation, but it was inspired speculation. From time to time it formed a framework for thinking in Western Europe and beyond until the beginning of the present century. But until the present century the existence of atoms hadn't been proved. It was only speculation.

In their speculation the Greeks may have been guided by logic or intuition or the use of analogy, yet certainly not by observation. Yet they arrived at a very useful take-off point for twentieth century scientists whose instruments made it possible to establish that the atom actually existed, and to bring it under control. In particular, by asserting that atoms were changeless the Greeks focussed attention on the question of time. Like the immortal gods, their atoms, being changless, were not subject to time. If there existed only one single atom in total isolation, time would have no meaning. Time would not even exist. The atom would be the only reality. If atoms are the only reality, all else must be a form of insubstantial pageantry that gathers and fades like puffs of smoke. All else would be, as the Buddhists put it, *Māra* – Illusion.

It is most important that ordinary people should have at least a clear outline picture of the world and the universe they live in, and not cling to 'flat earth' concepts. The revolution in thinking that is now required from the public, if quantum theory is to be properly assimilated, is greater than the revolution in thinking in the sixteenth century when people had to understand that if you sailed to the end of the world you wouldn't go over the edge and fall off. But the instruments for explanation are immensely improved. One difficulty is that specialists are not necessarily the best instructors for the dumb unmathematical, just as gifted musicians are not necessarily the best teachers for the musically untalented. In the next chapter, I, a person with little mathematics, will set out my picture of the universe in so far as, from the reading of books, I have been able to form one. From its shortcomings experts in the art of popular diffusion may perhaps learn where the common reader is likely to run into difficulties. Others may like to take it as a starting point and improve on it.

REFERENCE NOTES

Chapter 1.

1. The debates in ancient India concerning Being (*sat*) and Non-being (*asat*), are interestingly described by Debiprasad Chattopadhyaya in Mohammed Said, (1990), pp.49 ff.
2. But this may no longer be tenable, for it appears that a reflector telescope was used by Leonard Digges in England between 1540 and 1559. See *The Origins of the Reflecting Telescope*, Presidential Address to the British Astronomical Association, **101**, 6, 1991, p.335 ff. by Colin Ronan.
3. 'The Academician Ruan Yuan wrote in 1799: 'Father Benoist says that the sun is static and central in the universe. But this is totally different from what Father Schall wrote in 1640. How can the theories of this one and the same Westerner [Copernicus] be so self-contradictory?' For the next half century European science was discredited in Chinese eyes.' J.S. Cummins.
4. A.Koyré, (1957), p.275.
5. This was at Wealdstone, near London, on a multi-winged machine invented by F.H. Phillips.
6. The last couplet, written by Sir John Collins Squire, capped the epitaph intended for Sir Isaac Newton written by Alexander Pope.
7. H.G. Wells (1895), p.219 ff.
8. John Gribbin & Martin Rees, (1990), p.280.

2

From Flat Earth to Flat Universe

We will now make a journey in time from the year 1900 to the present, and survey the chasm which has opened up beneath our feet. It is just as important that we should come to terms on a lay level with nuclear physics, as it was in the age of Christopher Columbus that the ordinary thinking man should come to terms with the idea that the earth wasn't flat. This chapter aims at nothing more than to diminish Everyman's fear of nuclear physics (the mystery of mysteries which can blow the world to pieces!) by making familiar a few of the commonest terms and basic ideas, and then by setting out very briefly the most important names of people and events, marking the way from Copernicus to Chernobyl. Those who wish to go further may then read some of the books listed in the Bibliography which are written with the intention of introducing Everyman to cosmology and subatomic physics, beginning perhaps with James Hemming's *Instead of God*, and then coming to grips in more detail with physics in *The Cosmic Onion* by Frank Close, or the reader may prefer to start with the great questions which cosmology and subatomic physics provoke provided in Stephen Hawking's *A Brief History of Time: A Reader's Companion*.

Below the level of molecules at which we live and move there had long been suspected to exist another level of being, consisting of infinitely small particles of matter – the atoms. When it was found that some of these assumed atoms were emitting rays, and when the rays in cathode tubes were proved by J.J. Thomson at the end of the nineteenth century to consist of particles which could actually be weighed, it became clear that the atom not only existed but had a structure which could perhaps be dismantled. The exploration of the atom was carried out by brilliant minds in many different countries acting not as a team but in concert, regardless of national boundaries. By 1930 the exploration of the next level below the atom, that of the nucleus of the atom and its electrons, was under way. This age saw the development of nuclear physics, and the growing menace of the mushroom cloud.

The first machine capable of accelerating particles was built in Cambridge at the Cavendish laboratory between 1928 and 1932. From the 1950s onwards giant particle accelerators began to be built which could be used in fact as microscopes for subatomic investigation. At first only a few particles were known, for example up to 1932 just the photon, proton, electron and neutron. It was as if in an unknown script one had identified a few of the commonest letters such as 'e', 's', 'n' and 'r', without being aware of the extent of the alphabet yet to be discovered. Nor were the early researchers aware that the particles would fall into categories and classes, as the letters of the alphabet may be divided into vowels, consonants and so on. But now that the many particles known to us have been classified, it will be a great help to the common man in coming to terms with the changes which modern physics is imposing on our understanding of the universe, if we first get clear how the inhabitants of the subatomic world are classified.

My aim here is simply to summarise just enough of what needs to be known about physics and cosmology for the reader to have an idea of the developments during the last fifty years which have shaped our understanding of the universe we live in. It is not my intention to attempt to *explain* them. For this reason I do not attempt to explain the 'spin' of particles, which would greatly lengthen and complicate the chapter, though 'spin' is often an essential part of the definition of a term. The diagrams themselves embody the idea of 'spin', but the differences in 'spin' are simply shown with the terms. I shall try to compress important information in diagrams where possible. Diagrams can sometimes be misleading, but in the early stages of enquiry they are often helpful, even if needing to be modified or re-stated later.

First let us divide subatomic particles into two sorts – those which may be regarded as the building blocks of the universe, which are known as *fermions*, (see squares A and C in Figure 1), and those which 'carry' the forces which 'glue' them together, and which are known as *bosons*, (see squares B and D). The word *force* is a fiction, though a useful one. Isaac Newton would have had difficulty in describing universal gravitation without it. It is nevertheless a fiction useful for summarising the behaviour of certain particles. Today it is not unusual to speak of the 'interactions of particles' rather than of 'forces'. The 'strong force', for example, is the 'strong nuclear interaction'.

Under fermions or 'building blocks' we have in square A *protons* and *neutrons* which, when combined, form the nuclei of atoms. In square C are two main sorts of particles. They are referred to collectively as *quarks* and *leptons*. Quarks are believed to be the fundamental constituents of matter. Leptons are grouped in three families, each of which includes nearly massless particles called *neutrinos*. Leptons means 'light ones'. By contrast the neutron and proton particles in square A are referred to collectively as *baryons* or 'heavy ones'.

It will be noticed that it is almost impossible to talk about the world of particles in lay language without using rather wild metaphors; striking examples of this will be seen shortly, when the smallest of all particles, the quarks, are classified as red, blue or green, (some authors say yellow), though they have no literal colour; and the word *carry*, as used above, suggests that the particle has a force on its back which it transports from one place to another. The way in which a force is exerted seems to be, to borrow a useful metaphor, by one particle flinging a boson, a carrier particle, to another that receives it, in the manner of a medicine ball,[1] so that it donates an output of energy, and, if it can be imagined, the reverse case is when a particle receives an input of energy, 'stealing' it from another. Some particles, however, neither attract nor repel, but are neutral.

The fundamental distinction between fermions and bosons is that fermions are matter particles and bosons are force particles. When saying matter particles we are referring mainly to quarks and electrons, and when we speak of forces we are referring to the gravitational, electromagnetic, weak and strong nuclear forces. The strong force, however, is now regarded as a remnant of the 'colour' force or interaction between quarks. These forces are mediated through the agency of five different sorts of particle – *gravitons, photons, massive vector bosons, pions* and *gluons.*

The smallest of all particles so far known is called a *quark.* If an electric charge is administered to a quark it does not disintegrate into yet smaller particles, as occurred with the original splitting of the atom by Rutherford in 1919. The extra energy simply calls into being another similar quark. We may therefore begin with quarks and build up from there.

Two quarks or three may be held together by the 'colour' interaction which is mediated by the go-between particles called gluons. There are, however, two types of gluon, one 'weak', the other 'coloured'. The weak gluon holds together two quarks, which are subject to radioactive decay, and are therefore unstable. The particles so made are called *mesons*, and are shown in square B of Figure 1. The coloured gluon holds together three quarks which form a very stable group. This stable group is shown in square A of Figure 1, which we will now consider.

There are various sorts of quark with rather fascinating names. But we are concerned here with only two of the six groups – 'up-quarks' and 'down-quarks'. Each of these groups has three different sorts of quark particles described as red, blue and green. These combine in different ways, as shown in Figure 2, but the essential point is that one up-quark and two down-quarks held together by 'coloured gluons' make a neutron particle, and two up-quarks and one down-quark also held together by 'coloured gluons' make a proton. If one proton and one neutron come within range of each other and are held together by the strong nuclear force mediated by pions, you have the nucleus of a very basic kind of atom, deuterium. It remains then for one or more electrons to be attracted into orbit round a nucleus, and to start as it were circling the nucleus like planets circling the sun, for different types of atom to come into existence. If these different atoms held together by photons then combine in different ways forming molecules, the properties are ready for the drama of evolution to begin.

It would be interesting to describe the characteristics of other building-block particles, but this may be left for specialists. In the interests of simplification nothing has been said about the *spin* of particles, of the size of particles, or of the ways in which their behaviour seems to contradict the laws of common sense. For this the reader should turn to books whose concern is the world of the infinitely small, which is no less fascinating than the world of the infinitely large – inverted astronomy, as it were. But this minute world, as we said just now, is hard to present in general terms without the help of metaphors. It is difficult, for example, to conceive of the 'penetrating power' of a *neutrino*. We can imagine a cannon ball fired at point blank range into a

Figure 1

Sub-atomic Particles

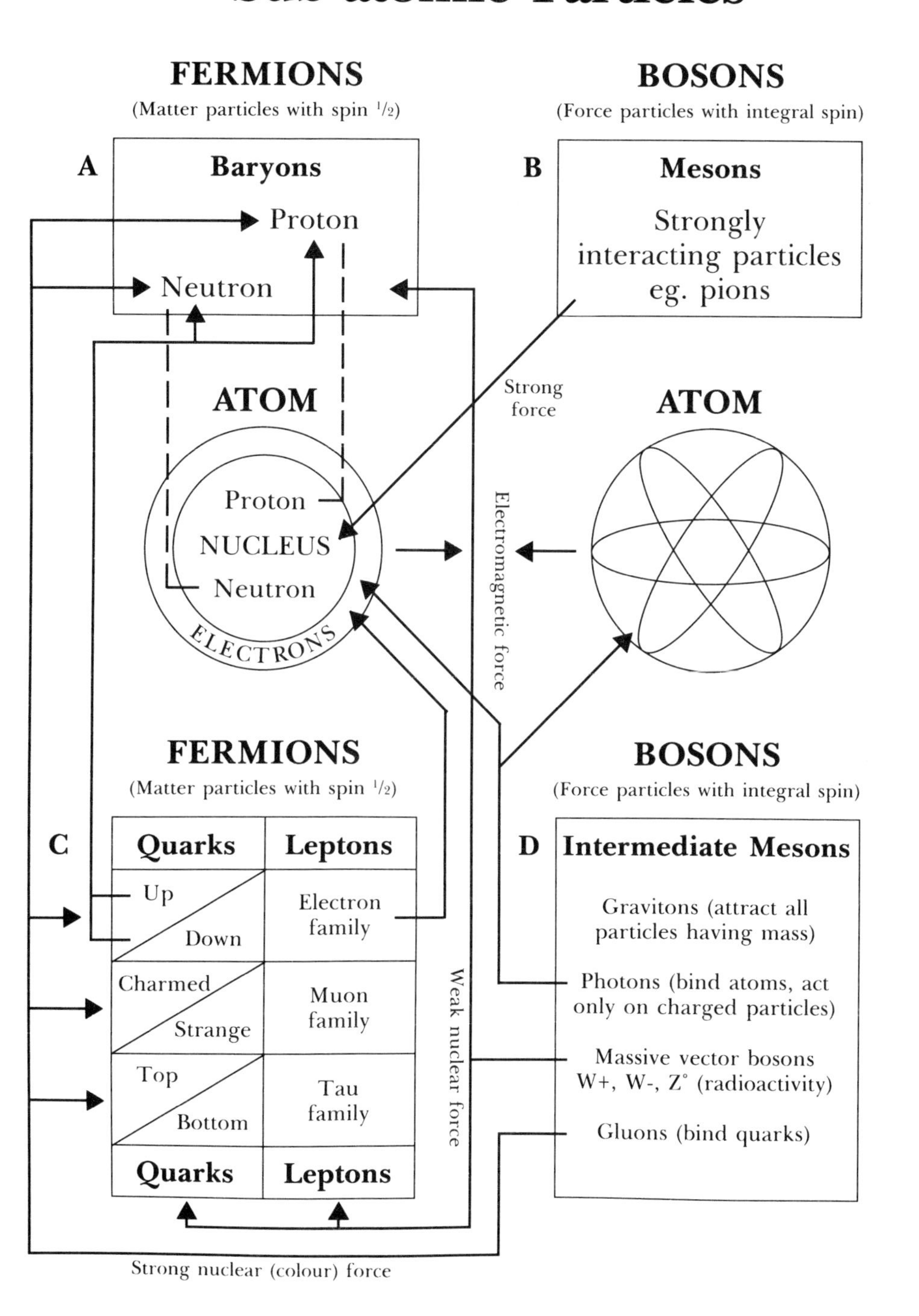

Figure 2
Quarks in Stable Groups

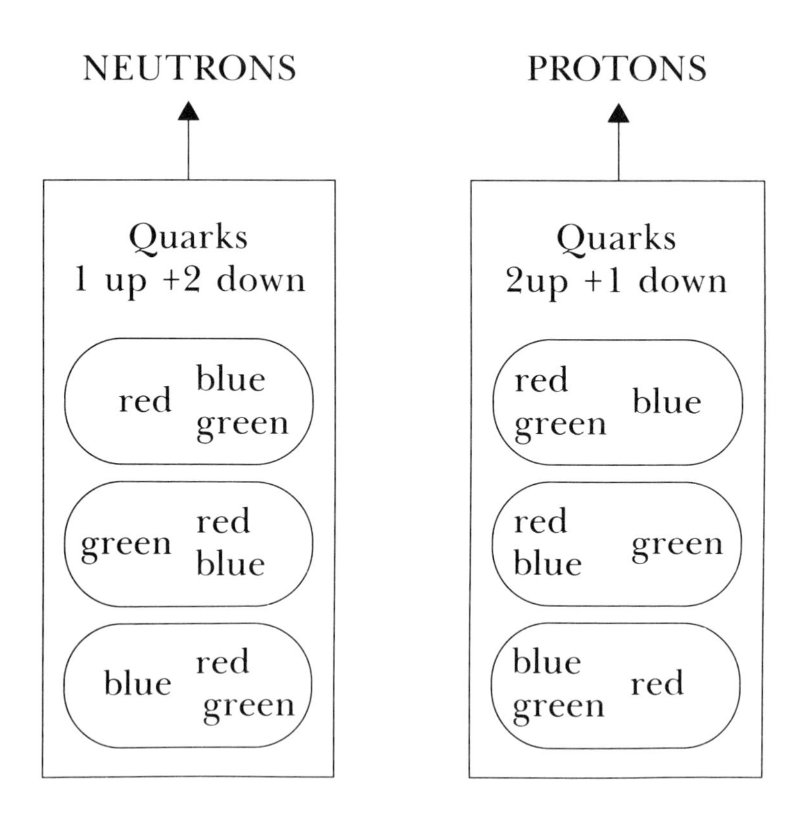

square of British infantry at the battle of Waterloo. The cannon ball tears its way through flesh and bone for some yards until it sags to earth and is stopped. But a neutrino fired from the sun is so small that it will enter the world, sail through the enormous 'gaps' in matter, and come out the other side 'untouched'. The unmathematical layman is forced again and again to use metaphor and analogy like crutches if he is to advance at all, though they are crutches which can easily let him down. Language must therefore be used with caution.

Let us now turn from the matter particles of square A in Figure 1 to square D, where the intermediate meson particles are shown. It would seem that they are called intermediate because they mediate between matter particles, transferring energy from one form of matter to another. This is done in four different ways, by means of the four fundamental forces of nature through the mediation of five main types of particle. Two of these types of particle operate over great distances, and three over minute distances. First we may consider the five types of particle themselves, and then review the four fundamental forces of nature.

There are three main types of particle which operate only at exceedingly short range. They are:

(a) Gluon particles, (see square D in Figure 1), which bind together quarks, and in particular the *up* and *down* quarks which form protons and neutrons.

(b) Pions or pi meson particles, (see square B) which bind together protons and neutrons to form the stable nucleus of the atom.

(c) Massive vector bosons known as W and Z particles, which transfer the energy which transmutes neutrons into proton, electron and neutrino particles, causing radiation of alpha, beta or gamma particles, i.e. they are responsible for radiation.

Then there are two types of particle which can operate not only at close range but over immense, even infinite distances. They are:

(d) Photons which interact only with electrically charged particles. They cause electrons to orbit the atom and they hold atoms together. The packets of energy discharged as photons are visible to the eye as light.

(e) Gravitons which carry gravitational force and affect every type of particle having mass.

The four 'forces' are usually listed in the reverse order, i.e., from weak to strong, as follows:

(1) The gravitational force, mediated by gravitons, the weakest force, but influencing mass particles over immense distances.

(2) The electromagnetic force, mediated by photons, and also capable of operating over immense distances.

(3) The weak nuclear force, mediated by massive vector bosons, and only operating at very small ranges.

(4) The strong force, mediated by gluons and pions at minute distances.

Let us now consolidate our survey so far. We began with the *fermion.* This term covered two types of 'building block', the heavy type or *baryon,* and the light type or *lepton.* Baryons are composed of *quarks* which are held together by the strong 'colour' force mediated by *gluons* to make *protons* and *neutrons.* These are held together by *pions* to form the *nucleus* of the *atom.* To the nucleus may be added one or more *electrons,* a type of lepton, which is not affected by the strong force, with the result that whereas the nucleus is held strongly together, electrons in an atom can be knocked out of orbit. This is a fact of great importance since, if electrons were not highly mobile we should not have the wonderful range of different atoms which have made possible the universe we inhabit. In addition we have encountered the *graviton,* the *photon, intermediate mesons,* including *massive vector bosons,* the strongly interacting *mesons* and *neutrinos.*

For the layman entering this field for the first time, there is a formidable vocabulary to be mastered. These seventeen words are only a beginning. Some of the words, like 'quark', are new inventions. Others, like 'particle', are so familiar that they do not appear to need learning. But on getting into the subject the meaning is found to be no longer familiar. Yet it is not the words themselves, but the behaviour of the things they summarise, that cause difficulty. The words 'atom' and 'particle' have been used for centuries, but not in the same senses as now. The photon and graviton are new words but not altogether unfamiliar to our experience. We are aware of the photon when we experience rays of sunlight. A beam of light consists of a stream of these particles to which the name of photon was first given by Albert Einstein. They carry energy, and under certain circumstances can impinge on an atom and cause it, by reason of its increase in energy, to throw out one of its orbiting electrons. We are also aware in a way of gravitons. Loosely speaking we are aware of them when we experience the gravitational pull of the earth. Strictly speaking, however, this is not correct, because the graviton is not involved in the normal 'pull of gravity' or weight, but only in the propagation of changes to a gravitational field. If the space between the nucleus of an atom and the electron or electrons which 'circle' it is thought of as a void or vacuum, this vacuum contains the possibility of new quantum particles, new quanta, being formed as soon as sufficient energy is supplied. If the energy supplied is not enough to create a real particle, there may yet be enough to create a 'virtual particle', one which comes into existence with its paired antiparticle, and then instantly ceases to exist. Each type of matter particle has a corresponding antiparticle. When a particle collides with its antiparticle, they annihilate, leaving only energy.[2]

Since what has been described is in a way the alphabet of subatomic physics, it may be helpful to summarise it using a different angle of attack. Familiar substances such as wood or metal or meat are composed of molecules. Molecules are themselves composed of atoms, of which there are approximately a hundred different sorts, such as hydrogen, carbon or sulphur. Atoms are composed of particles. At the sub-atomic level particles are of two sorts – 'building-block' particles named fermions, and 'gluing' or 'cementing' particles named bosons.

Let us first concentrate on the building-block particles and follow them 'downwards'. Here we find the 'massive building-block' particles known as baryons. They are of two sorts – protons and neutrons, which form the nucleus of the atom.

Now, if we go down to a 'lower' level yet, we find 'light building-blocks', from which protons and neutrons are themselves constructed. These are of two sorts, namely quarks of the up/down variety, and leptons which exist in three families. From the electron family come the electron particles which may link to an atomic nucleus and, according to the number of electrons doing so, help to create different sorts of atom.

What holds the particles together? What is the binding force? The exerting of 'force' is a transferring of energy from one particle to another. Particles which do this are called bosons. They 'glue' or 'cement' particles together. Which particles do this depends on the properties of the boson and whether the building-block particles have electric charges or not.

Now let us trace the bosons back in conjunction with the blocks that they glue together. At the level of quarks and leptons we have four sorts of particle collectively known as intermediate mesons. These are called gluons, photons, massive vector bosons and gravitons.

The *gluons* are carriers of the very strong force known as the 'colour' force. They operate on quarks, binding them together in groups of three to make massive building-blocks, baryons.

Photons are particles which transfer energy to and from electrons, and carry the electromagnetic force which holds them around the atomic nucleus and which also binds separate atoms together.

Massive vector bosons is the collective name for three particles which carry the weak nuclear force, namely W plus, W minus and the neutral Z boson particles. They have a rôle in the behaviour of neutrino particles and radioactivity, but this is outside the scope of the present brief summary.

Gravitons are the particles which transfer gravitational force to all matter. All matter is attracted by their action, which, though weak, operates over immense distances, and collectively with great force.

Rising now to the level of the massive building-blocks, the protons and neutrons, we find particles collectively known as mesons. Of these the *pion* is of vital importance, since it is this particle which binds together protons and neutrons to form a stable nucleus of the atom.

Such is the strange world of particles. It seems a thousand years removed from the seventeenth century when Descartes and Henry More debated the omnipotence of God, stating that 'as matter is always divisible, it is clear that God will never be able to bring this division to its end and that there will always be something which evades His omnipotence.'[3] Whether the quark can or cannot itself be divided into something smaller cannot perhaps be known with absolute certainty. The inputs of energy used today may be inadequate and in future centuries may seem quite trivial. A theory is always tentative.[4] A huge readjustment in living and thinking, however, is now inevitable, as a result of the quantum theory which led on to the 'uncertainty principle' first formulated by Heisenberg in 1926. We ourselves are concerned with only a minute part of all that is, minute in time as well as in space. The sheer size and grandeur of the thing is intimidating. What saves us from despair is the fact that throughout the universe there appears to be a pattern. Pattern is not purpose, however. One of the aims of science is to explore the patterns formed by the processes of all that is – to explore the Tao. But the explorations of nuclear physicists have now distanced modern ideas of the universe as far from those of the Victorian Age as the Victorian Age was from the Stone Age.

In ancient times men thought of the world as being intermediate between several heavens and hells. We still speak of being 'in the seventh heaven'. According to our present knowledge we exist as thinking animals at the fifth or intermediate level of organisation out of a total of nine levels. (See Figure 3). But the underlying reality of the whole cosmos consists in sets of oscillating fields of energy. The oscillations can be read as 'waves', whose crests represent concentrations of energy, described as 'particles'. The intensity of the field at any point gives an indication of the statistical probability of finding a particle at that point. It does not indicate that a particle exists at that point, but only that at that point the field may be manifesting the probability of a concentration of energy. Each particle has its own field, and one type of field, under certain conditions, reacts on another. This is done by the interchange of quantum particles of the gluon type. Such interchanges occur when there is compatibility. This meeting of compatibles is, however, believed to occur by chance, and not according to a law or pattern. If the universe may be thought of as engaged in a cosmic dance, though chance promotes the encounters which create the dance, the mathematics underlying the behaviour of the partners in the dance indicate that the dance is patterned. We have therefore a patterned cosmos based on randomness. It was this that led some physicists to say that God plays dice!

It has been believed that when our universe began there was so high a concentration of energy that, to quote Heinz R. Pagels' admirably concise and vivid description, 'The four interactions were unified as one highly-symmetrical interaction. As this fireball of swirling quarks, coloured gluons, electrons, and photons expanded, the universe cooled and the perfect symme-

Figure 3

The Nine Levels of Organisation

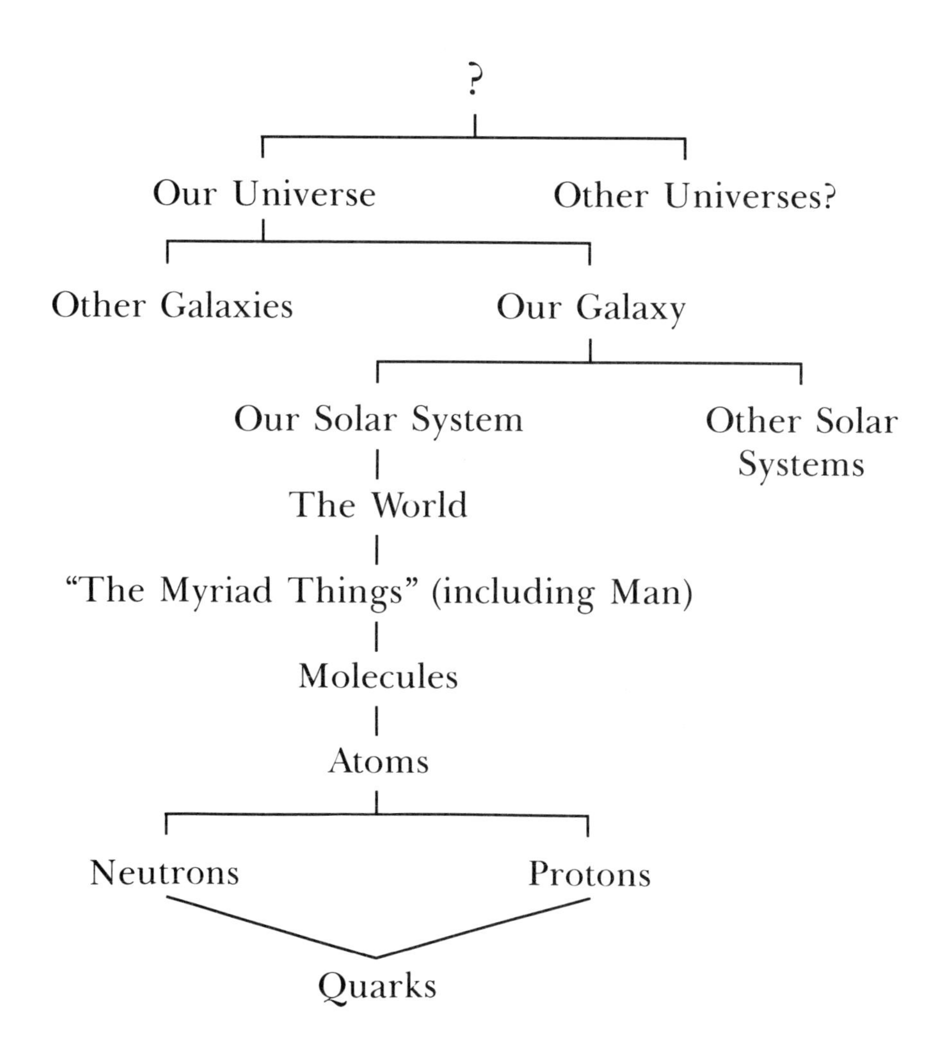

try began to break. First gravity was distinguished from the other interactions, and then the strong, weak, and electromagnetic interactions became apparent as they froze out of the cooling universe, manifesting symmetry breaking. Exotic quanta like charmed particles, (see Figure 1, square C), decayed away, and soon mostly protons, neutrons, electrons, photons and neutrinos were all that was left. After still further cooling, atoms could form and condense into stars; galaxies developed and planets emerged. As the surface temperatures of some planets dropped, complex molecules began to form – the building blocks for life. Even in the evolution of life we see this process of symmetry breaking at work as organisms generally evolved from simple to more complex ones . . . Our world manifests a broken or imperfect symmetry. But out of that imperfection arose the possibility of life.'[5] (See Figure 4.)

This, in its brief and simplified form, was how, until quite recently, informed people viewed the universe and its origin. But cosmology does not stand still, and fresh discoveries about the nature of outer space have led to new thinking on the subject, which may now be summarised.

As Gribbin and Rees put it, 'Most of the universe is empty space, filled with a weak background sea of electromagnetic radiation, with a temperature of 3 degrees above the absolute zero of temperature, which lies at -273 degrees C.'[6] How difficult it is, even in this sort of description, to avoid poetic language! The metaphorical sea seems to be whispering to us from the remotest shores.They even suggest that universes may exist like froth or bursting bubbles on the shore of some timeless sea, as was said in the previous chapter, p.23. Argument developed in the 1950s about whether the universe was in a Steady State, with new galaxies being continually formed from new matter, or whether it was created by a Big Bang. The Steady State theory had to be abandoned, but the Big Bang conclusion can lead to two main theories. In one, the universe was created out of nothing: all mass was

Figure 4

Cosmological Evolution

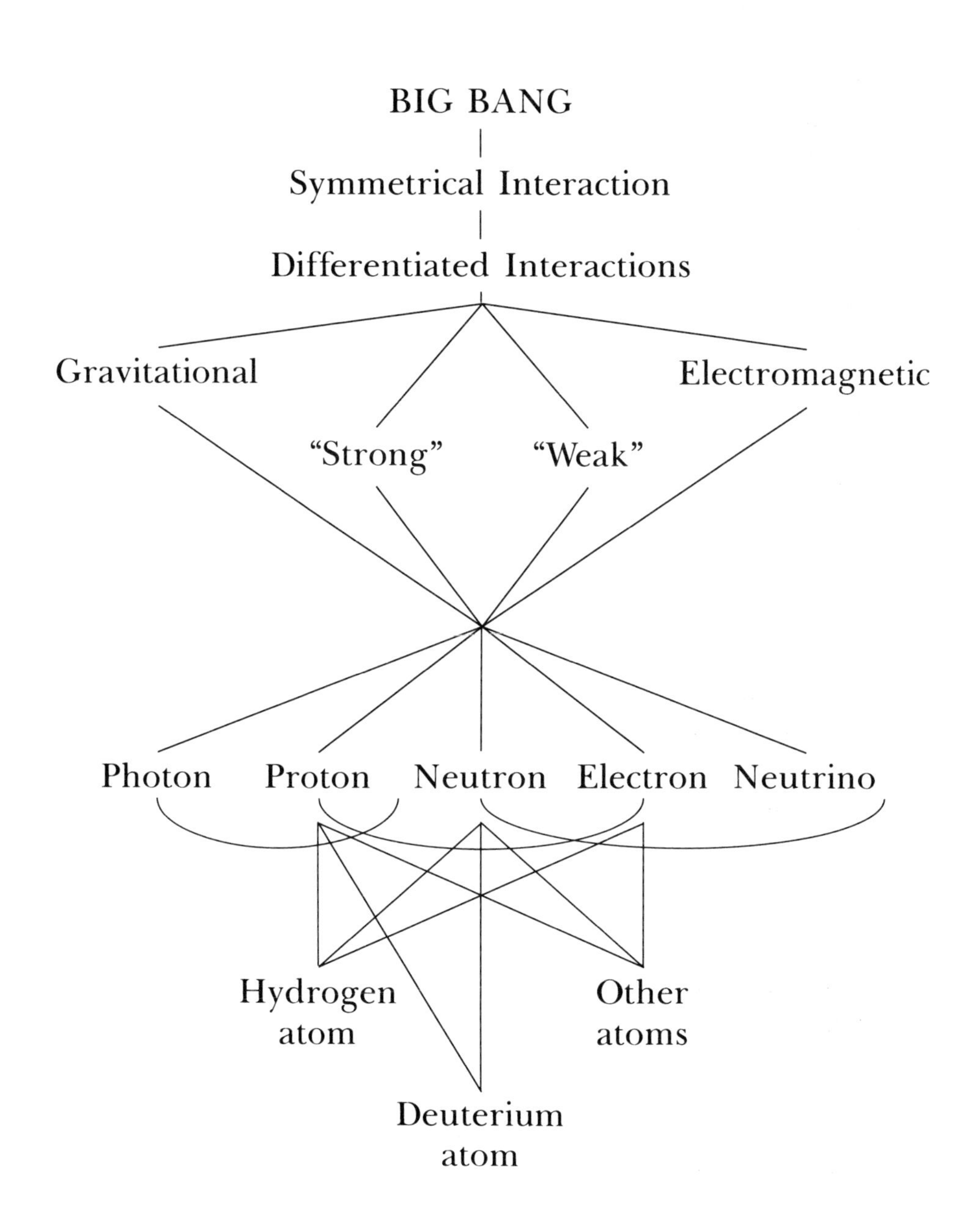

contained in a zero volume (a 'singularity' where all the known laws of physics and matter are suspended), and exploded. The universe was thus created and time 'began'. The universe is still rushing outward, and may or may not eventually be pulled back on itself by gravity, leading to the Big Crunch, the compression of all matter into no volume, and the end of time.

In the second, the usual concept of time is replaced by 'imaginary time', (based on the use of the square root of -1, a legitimate mathematical tool of analysis), leading to a 'flat universe'.[7] In this case although the universe may expand and contract, it does so without starting from or collapsing into a zero volume – there is no singularity. In this theory expounded by Hawking there are no edges to space or time, but neither are these dimensions infinite. (Hawking likens them to the surface of an orange with no ends or beginnings – but with finite dimensions.)

It was then realised that whether the universe is going to expand for ever or to collapse again is a matter of calculation. One needs to find out how much matter there is in the universe, and from that to calculate whether there is enough to cause everything eventually to fall back again into one immense concentration of matter-energy, or so little that all the constituents of all the galaxies will be expanding for ever.

The upshot of this enquiry was that the matter-energy throughout space which can be detected amounts to no more than 10% of the total to be expected even for the open universe! 90% of the universe must be composed of something described as Cold Dark Matter (C.D.M.), the stuff which forms density peaks by which energy is realised. But it is not yet known what C.D.M. is.

Much reflection has also been given to the realisation that our universe would not have been possible had there not been a micro-fine adjustment of the factors which control density. So delicate is the tuning that it could not be the result of chance. The question therefore arises: Was our universe designed by a Creator, or is it that a universe can only come into existence if such fine tuning is inherent in the laws of physics which control it? With no such fine tuning – no universe; all others would abort – either collapse or never emerge. This is the great unanswered question. For some the existence of a Creator seems obvious, for others not, but rather that it is natural, and that if a universe can only appear under certain conditions, it is under those conditions that it must appear.

When I first began to appreciate the immensity and beauty and mystery of the universe I compared it in my mind to a celestial cathedral. There seemed to be a sense of design and harmony and organisation in it such as one observes in great cathedrals. But then I found I was being ensnared by metaphor. For just as a cathedral is brought into being by some great architect, so, one would suppose, has the cathedral of the universe been brought into being by some creator, some supreme intelligence. This sort of reasoning is fallacious. What cathedral extends for myriad light year after myriad light year? In what cathedral does one find foundries spewing out or spinning the raw materials for better worlds, while in another part humans like small gnats 'wail in doleful choir'? In what cathedral does one find the church furniture, vestments, passing worshippers, random bric-à-brac, sucked down into the crypt or into countless crypts, there to be compressed into such tiny volumes that there is even the possibility that they occupy no volume at all? The universe is no cathedral. Metaphors which momentarily illumine on human scale one tiny aspect of the Tao are grotesquely limiting and must be discarded as soon as their brief moment of illumination has done its work. Otherwise our minds become entangled in cosmic spiders' webs from which it is difficult to get clear. *'Tao k'o tao, pu ch'ang tao.'* 'The Tao which can be described in words is not the eternal Tao.'[8]

In our present state of knowledge there are a great many open questions, and extreme humility seems called for. It would be unworthy of Man, or insulting to his Creator, for an antagonist to assume that his opinion is necessarily correct. With the human species still behaving most of the time as animals programmed for survival it will be surprising, however, if those who advocate tolerance and reason, or who happen to be a minority, do not from time to time find themselves segregated for butchery. How often this has happened in the past.

If this life is to be understood we must come to terms with its paradoxes. The basic fact is that the ancient dream of the alchemists has been realised. Matter is mutable, not, as they believed, by the application of gentle heat such as is used in the hatching of eggs, but by the application of huge amounts of energy. With particles which have electric charges it is also possible to create antimatter, a particle of antimatter having the same mass as a particle of matter, but the opposite charge. Mass is a form of energy. Energy arrives not in a continuous stream, but in 'packets' or quanta. Quanta behave like particles, impinging on things, as we know from the reaction of our skin to an overdose of photons when sunbathing. Particles are also probability waves. They do not exist at certain points, but have a tendency to be found there, or alternatively they have a tendency to occur at certain times. These possibilities can be charted as waves. An object is therefore not a solid object but a pattern of probabilities, which are, however, probabilities of interconnections taking place. The universe, therefore, does not consist at bottom of the sort of basic building blocks which Democritus imagined, but of a pulsating web of interconnections. The observer of nature is part of this web, and no objective description is possible, because he is himself a part of what he is observing.

Our belief in the purpose of the universe, our understanding of how it is composed and our interpretation of experience, was found to be based on no secure foundation. At first it was based on scriptural authority, then, when this was challenged, on the mechanistic operations of solid matter, and now on a randomly vibrating nexus of fields in which the fluctuations of energy manifest themselves in the ceaseless creation and annihilation of particles and virtual particles, and in which the comprehensible philosophy of determinism has been partly replaced by one based on probabilities and chance. This has, over the centuries, had the effect of undermining the intellectual and moral basis of society. A loss of confidence may be traced back to the fifteenth century when the old certainties began to fall away. Its early impact is most vividly shown in the paintings of Hieronymus Bosch.

One by one since 1905 the planks on which we stood have been removed. For a moment we looked down into the chasm below, and then began to drop. Artists and poets were perhaps the first to react to the insecurity. Is it surprising that in a disintegrating world the human body should have been portrayed with two faces, or made of clockwork or bits from the scrap heap, or like a boulder with holes in it, or like a bag full of surgical offal? What more appropriate to the age in which the randomness of the universe was discovered than that the artists should express themselves by covering their canvasses with random drops or splashes of paint? Or that words should be strung together at random, or in contradictory structures, or in scintillating constellations in which every word interacts with every other word? Is it surprising that the scientist who presented the world with its first artificial fertiliser should also have presented his country with mustard gas to be used immediately against his fellow Europeans? Or that this should be followed step by frightful step to the ultimate bomb? Yet it really doesn't matter to the Tao. There are myriads of other worlds where things may be handled better. Some will succeed and some will fail. It is a matter of statistical probability.

When the bottom drops out of the world, people clutch whatever looks solid enough to give them support. But falling can be turned to flying. Our task is not to clutch blindly at things, but in the dream of life to learn to fly. For this two things must be done. First we must make a cool appraisal of the beliefs which have come down to us from the Bronze Age, to which we readily return when the going gets rough. The right to doubt must not be abandoned. There must be no loss of nerve this time, as there was following the defeat of Athens by Sparta in that first rational age.[9] Then we must come to grips with this great revolution in thought which is modern physics. Today it is as baffling for most people as was that earlier revolution when men discovered that the world was roughly spherical and not flat. In a few hundred years children will take our discoveries for granted. To find a way through the labyrinth of modern physics it is useful to be able to follow a thread. With such a thread we will close the present chapter. This thread is simply a string of names with a short description of an event and its date. Naturally there is no attempt to explain what has happened in the last four centuries, but merely to draw attention to some of the key names. Anyone who wishes to get a better understanding of this great revolution may consult some of the books suggested,[10] but it is also helpful, in finding one's way about in unfamiliar territory, to read biographies of the people who made the going, the main actors in the drama. Such a thread is admittedly a makeshift, because it attributes to one person what is often the work of many, and it leaves out the names of scores of others who made important contributions. Nevertheless, a string may be a lifeline.

KEY EVENTS IN THE DEVELOPMENT OF MODERN PHYSICS

1514 Copernicus proposes heliocentric model of the solar system.

1609 Galileo observes the four major moons of Jupiter with the newly invented telescope, and describes the laws of free-falling bodies.

1618 Grimaldi discovers interference and diffraction of light waves.

1632 Galileo introduces the concept of relativity to physics.
1650 From about now valves, indispensable for much machinery, begin to be developed from lock gates for controlling hydraulic systems. Early inventors unknown.
1675 Roemer estimates the velocity of light from observations of Jupiter's satellites in eclipse at different distances. Discovers that light travels at a finite but very high speed.
1687 Newton publishes *Philosophiae Naturalis Principia Mathematica.*
1704 Newton publishes his *Optics*, giving spectral analysis of white light.
1729 Gray discovers transmission of electricity over distance.
1746 Masschenbroek and von Kleist invent leiden jars, leading to electric batteries and accumulators.
1748 Lomonosov establishes laws of conservation of mass and energy.
1755 Kant proposes the origin of the sun and planets from a nebula.
1770s Galvani studies electricity in relation to animals' muscles.
1781 Kant in his *Critique of Pure Reason* asks whether the universe is limited in space and had a beginning in time.
1785 Coulomb measures the force acting between two stationary electric charges in a vacuum (electrostatic force).
1798 Cavendish measures the gravitational attraction between two lead weights, determines mass of the earth and value of gravitational constant.
1803 Young demonstrates the wave theory of light.
1808 Dalton propounds his atomic theory.
1820 Ampère works on laws of electromagnetism.
1825 Laplace publishes his *Mécanique céleste,* offering fully determinist explanation of the universe.

1830 Faraday discovers induction.
1831 Faraday invents first dynamo.
1834 Clapeyron develops second law of thermodynamics.
1842 Doppler observes change in pitch of sound when its source varies in distance from the observer. (Doppler effect later applied to the interpreting of spectral changes of stars in judging direction of their movement.)
1857 Kircher at work on propagation of electrical conductors.
1859 Kircher discovers that the ratio of absorption and emissive power of electromagnetic radiation is a universal function of wavelength and temperature.
1860 Kircher lays foundations of spectral analysis.
1861 Angström analyses the sun's spectrum.
1862 de Chancourtois notices periodicity in the properties of elements.
1863 Maxwell demonstrates mathematically the existence of electromagnetic 'waves'.
1865 Faraday and Maxwell introduce the idea of a 'field of force'. Maxwell produces theory unifying the partial theories describing the forces of electricity and magnetism.
1867 Riemann evolves non-Euclidean geometry.
1868 Angström publishes *Recherches sur le spectre solaire.*
1872 Mendeleev proposes Periodic Table of Elements.
1874 Stoney introduces the word 'electron' and estimates its charge.
1879 Crookes postulates that cathode rays are a stream of particles carrying negative electric charges.
1886 Hertz discovers photo-electric effect, (ejection of electrons from certain metal surfaces when light falls on them).
1887 Michelson and Morley carry out experiments in measuring the speed of light, with no evidence for the existence of the ether.

1888 Hertz demonstrates electromagnetic 'waves' in the 'ether', supporting Maxwell's theory of electromagnetic propagation.
Thomson identifies the particles ejected from certain metals as being the same as exist in cathode rays.
1894 Thomson investigates cathode rays. Oliver Lodge sends signals without wires using 'Hertzian waves'.
1895 Roentgen discovers that 'X-rays' are generated in a vacuum tube similar to the cathode ray tube. Marconi evolves method of propagating and receiving 'Hertzian waves'.
1896 Becquerel notices that photographic plates are blackened by 'radiation' from uranium, i.e. the effects of radioactivity are observed.
1897 Thomson identifies the electron as 'corpuscles' which cause the 'flow' of electricity by convection of negative charge. The term 'electron' now established.
1898 The Curies discover radioactivity in thorium and in two new elements, 'polonium' and 'radium'.
Marconi sends messages over a distance of 12 miles.
1899 First wireless telegraphic message passed between England and France.
1900 Planck shows that a body can only emit or absorb light in integral multiples of the basic amount or quantum and not continuously. This leads to the quantum theory.
1902 Rutherford and Soddy discover that atoms are transformed by radioactive radiation, i.e. transmutation.
Kelvin puts forward the first experiment-based model for structure of the atom.
1905 Einstein explains photo-electric effect by means of the concept of quanta. Also publishes papers on 'the special theory of relativity', concluding that the speed of light is the upper limit to speed, and that the mass of a body increases when its speed increases. He also

suggests that mass and energy are interchangeable. The idea of the ether is no longer necessary.

1909 Rutherford and Royds prove that alpha particles are the nuclei of helium atoms.

Millikan measures the charges of electrons, and also finds that the mass of an electron is 1/1840 of the mass of a hydrogen atom.

1910 Rutherford studies the structure of atoms by observing the scattering of alpha particles when passing through thin metal foil.

1911 Rutherford publishes his model of a small heavy nucleus surrounded by light electrons.

1912 Wilson builds the first cloud chamber for particle detection.

1913 Niels Bohr proposes that electrons do not lose energy unless they jump to an orbit closer to the nucleus.

Geiger develops a machine capable of recording the passing of a single particle. (The Geiger-Muller tube.)

1915 Einstein proposes his General Theory of Relativity. Gravity is seen as a consequence of the fact that space-time is curved.

1916 Schwartchild solves equations describing Black Holes, using Einstein's General Theory of Relativity.

1919 Eddington verifies that in Einstein's General Theory of Relativity gravitation has an effect on photons though they have no mass, by observing that light from stars was deflected by the sun during the solar eclipse of 29th March.

1921 Hubble declares the universe to be expanding.

1922 Compton confirms the dual (particle/wave) nature of light by showing that photons lose momentum after colliding with electrons, and that this increases the wavelength.

Friedmann shows that the universe is unlikely to be static.

1923 De Broglie maintains that particles must have wave properties, just as light has particle properties.

1924 Pauli formulates the principle that no two electrons in an atom can have identical sets of quantum numbers. The same principle explains how the nucleus of an atom can be populated by particles at different energy levels. (Pauli's 'exclusion principle'.)

Hubble demonstrates that ours is not the only galaxy.

1925 Heisenberg, Jordan and Born evolve 'matrix mechanics' as a new version of the quantum theory, relying on what can be measured. Dirac reformulates this in a more generalised form as a coherent axiomatic theory.

1926 Einstein cannot accept non-determinacy. '*He* does not play dice.'

Heisenberg formulates the 'uncertainty principle' that the light by which a particle is detected will itself disturb that particle and change its velocity in a way which cannot be predicted.

1927 Lemaître rediscovers Friedmann's non-static universe.

Heisenberg develops Uncertainty Principle. (Impossibility of accurately determining simultaneously both the position and velocity of a particle.)

1928 Dirac predicts the existence of the positron, (positively charged antiparticle of the electron), and explains why matter particles have a 'spin' of 1/2.

1928-1932 Cockcroft builds the first machine for accelerating particles.

1929 Weyl asks why protons in atoms don't disintegrate.

Hubble demonstrates the expansion of the universe.

1930 Bothe and Becker discover that if light elements are exposed to alpha rays they emit a strong uncharged radiation.

1932 Irene Curie and Frederic Joliot show that this must be a new type of neutral particle that is radiated. Chadwick determines the mass of the new particle now named the neutron.

Anderson discovers positively charged particle (positron) with same mass as electron among cosmic ray particles.

1933-1936 Anderson and Neddermeyer find positive and negative particles with unusual powers of penetration in cosmic rays (i.e. mesons).

1934 Cerenkov makes possible a new particle-counter based on the discovery that light of characteristic properties is emitted when a charged particle moves in a substance at speed greater than the speed of light can be in that substance.

Chadwick and Goldhaber provide experimental support for the belief that the constituents of the nucleus are bound together by some 'nuclear force'.

Artificial radioactivity discovered by Curie-Joliot team, (leading to bombardment of nuclei by neutrons, and splitting of the nucleus).

1935 Yukawa publishes his theory on the nuclear force which binds the nucleons together in the nucleus. He claimed that as the electric field can produce photons, so the field of the strong force around the nucleus can produce some kind of particles.

1937 Blau and Wambacher discover that grains of silver halide in film are blackened by fast particles as well as by light.

1938-1939 Neddermeyer and Anderson, and Blackett and Wilson, work out the mass of particles heavier than electrons and lighter than protons, believed to be carriers of the strong force, and created when protons of the primary cosmic radiation encounter atomic nuclei in the upper atmosphere. Name of meson given to them.

1942 Fermi builds the first nuclear pile in Chicago.

1945 Powell and Occhialini expose photographic plates at high altitudes and show experimentally that the pion is created by collision of cosmic particles with atoms composing air, and that the product of these collisions is the muon. The muon decays into the electron, neutrinos also being emitted.

First atomic bombs dropped on Hiroshima and Nagasaki.

1946 Marshak and Bethe get credit for 'theory of two mesons', in which muons and pions are distinguished. But this had already been published in Japanese by Sakata and Inoue in 1943.

1947 Conversi, Pancini and Piccioni publish results of experiments measuring absorption of mesons in various nuclei.

Rochester and Butler present first clear results of cosmic particles appearing in cloud chambers. V tracks first observed, indicating existence of 'strange' particles.

Discovery of the pion by Powell.

1948 Bondi, Gold and Hoyle produce the steady state theory.

1949 Fermi and Yang investigate binding mechanism of baryons from triplets, and propose model which regarded pions as composed of nucleons and their antiparticles. Yukawa correctly predicts existence of meson.

1950 Carlson, Hooper and King obtain tracks on photographic plates at height of 21 km from which the energy and direction of photons resulting from impact of protons from cosmic rays impinging on the plate may be calculated.

1952 Glaser and Alvarez develop bubble chamber. Pais points out that 'strange' particles are never produced as singles, but usually in pairs.

The cosmotron accelerator inaugurated in the USA.

1953 Gell-Mann and Nishijima propose independently that a certain quantum number, termed 'strangeness', [S], exists, which is conserved in strong and electro-magnetic but not in weak interactions.

1955 Anti-proton first observed by Chamberlain and Segré. Russians build accelerator at Dubna.

1956 Sakata proposes model in which hadrons are composed of combinations of six known particles – neutron, proton, lambda and their antiparticles.

Cowan and Reines report discovery of neutrinos emitted by a reactor.

Shockley and colleagues awarded Nobel prize for developing first junction transistor.

1956-1957 Lee Tsung-Dao and Chen Ning-Yang conclude that parity in weak interactions might not be conserved, and that nature differentiates between Left and Right. (Application of P principle, i.e. parity or mirror inversion.)

1959 Regge explains most resonances as excited states of the lower-energy systems.

1960 First 28-GeV proton synchroton completed near Geneva (CERN).

First laser made by Maiman in 1960.

1960s and 1970s Hundreds of short-lived particles added to list of those known. Almost all were strong interaction particles.

1963-1967 First electron-positron storage rings inaugurated in Italy, France, USA. and USSR.

1964 Cronin and Fitch show that certain interactions are not invariant when the P principle and the C principle (changing particles into antiparticles) are applied together in a decay process. It followed that the T principle (time reversal) is also not absolute in conserving invariance. Invariance of interactions is only absolute

when all three principles – T, C and P apply conjointly.
Gell-Mann and Zweig suggest that all strong interaction particles are composed of quarks, (three fundamental particles and three antiparticles).

1965 Penzias and Wilson detect microwaves from beyond our galaxy. Steady-state theory no longer tenable? Penrose proves that any local region of the universe trapped by a horizon must develop a 'hole', i.e. a space-time singularity.
Feynman, Schwinger and Tomonaga develop Quantum Electro-Dynamics (QED).

1965-1970 Early development of the 'string theory'.

1967 Weinberg and Abdus Salam combine the electromagnetic and weak nuclear forces in an integrated mathematical description.

1968 Van der Meer develops 'stochastic cooling' for the CERN collider, which reduces the random motion of antiprotons (concentrates them) before further acceleration.
John Wheeler coins the term 'Black Holes'.

Early 1970s Second generation storage rings built.

1974 Hawking shows that Black Holes produce particles and themselves slowly evaporate.
Scherk and Schwartz further develop string theory.

Late 1970s Third generation storage rings built.

1981 The first proton/anti-proton collisions achieved at CERN.

1983 Massive vector boson particles or weak force carriers discovered at CERN, and the sixth (t) quark.

1984 First tevatron (1000 GeV accelerator) in action at Fermilab, Chicago.

Schwartz and Green revive interest in string theory, leading to heterotic string theory.

1986 Chernobyl atomic power station disaster.

REFERENCE NOTES

Chapter 2.

1. The metaphor of the medicine ball is gratefully borrowed from Ne'eman and Kirsh (1986), p.75. The authors say: 'It is easy to understand how the exchange of photons generates a repulsive force: think of two persons who play with a heavy ball by passing it to each other. Every time one of them catches the ball, he feels that he is pushed backward.' They go on to say that it is not so easy to explain the attractive force by analogy. For that one needs mathematics.
2. Hawking (1988), Glossary.
3. Koyré (1957), p.113.
4. On this see Hawking (1988), pp. 167 and 173.
5. Pagels, Heinz (1983), pp. 263–4.
6. Gribbin and Rees, (1990), p.6.
7. For details of the Flat Universe proposal see Hawking (1988), pp. 135–141.
8. This is the opening sentence of the great Taoist classic, the *Tao Tê Ching.*
9. On the Greek 'loss of nerve' see below, ch.3, p.58.
10. See the Bibliography under Barrow & Silk, Close, Davies, Gribbin & Rees, Hawking (1988) and (1992), Ne'eman & Kirsh, Pagels, Polkinghorne.

3

The Unacceptable Face of Christianity

Now, at the end of the twentieth century, we find ourselves poised, not, as in previous ages, between heaven and hell, but at a certain level in the organisation of matter. This matter, we find, ranges in its organisation from that which is utterly immense to that which is so minute that both are far beyond the scale of our visual imagination. Seen from another point of view, 'we' inhabit two worlds at the same time, the subatomic, which is random and immune to time as we know it, and the atomic and molecular, which is forever changing, and reasonably predictable. Ever since Man achieved intelligence he has been obsessed with prediction and the recognition of patterns, for without some ability to predict, life is likely to be particularly short.

Few things are more difficult or disagreeable than abandoning patterns we recognise and like, in order to learn new ones; under pressure we exchange one world picture for a different one; from the clash of ideas we find ourselves obliged to abandon beliefs in the virtues of our mother tongue, our food habits, our inherited myths, our prejudices and religious beliefs, and our idea of the world as a fairly stable and reasonable place where we know our way around, for a new one where nothing seems certain, and where rapid adaptation is essential for survival. Yet this is exactly what the entire human race must now do, and fast! When the changes seem overwhelming, or the pace of change is too rapid, there may well be a reaction. Such a reaction seems to have overtaken the Ancient Greeks when they had lost their democracies and when their great days were over. Gilbert Murray described it as 'loss of nerve'. Having come so near to our modern understanding of the solar system, they experienced a reaction against this sort of 'impiety', and the Mediterranean world suffered a mass movement back into mystery religion. The traditional pattern of West Asian and European thinking derived from a belief in a creator god has indeed proved itself to be exceedingly durable.

This pattern first took shape some 5,000 years ago, and has been in full vigour for the last three thousand. To break it will require the enlightened efforts of educated mass populations over several centuries. All too often attempts to 'break out' too far or too fast produce the kind of reaction Gilbert Murray described. Some features of the pattern appear to be shared by all the Indo-European and Semitic civilisations, while other features are limited to particular regions.

The first feature of the mould which shapes and patterns what may loosely be described as 'Western' thought, is the belief that the world, and indeed the entire universe, was *created.* In other parts of the world where thought is formed in a different mould, this is by no means self-evident, and people believe with equal conviction either that the world was always there, or that it happened naturally and spontaneously.

Those who believe that the world was created are logically compelled by the rules of their language to believe that there must therefore be a creator. Certain languages powerfully reinforce the primitive idea that if something happens it is because somebody did it. If a tree falls and kills a man, it didn't just happen. It occurred because somebody wished it to happen.

Behind every event there is a person. Even behind such ordinary words as 'living creatures' there lurks the idea of a creator who created his creatures. If the language spoken by people whose thinking is cast in this mould is one in which words are given special endings to indicate whether a person is male or female, as when we say actor or actress, then a person's attitude to the creation of the universe will also be moulded by whether the creation is attributed to a creator or a creatrix. People whose languages do not behave in this way are not subject to the same sort of pressures. Those who do speak such languages have to make a great effort to break away from the tyranny of words, as when supporters of Women's Lib refer to God as She. To be consistent they have to say: 'Goddess so loved the world that She gave Her only conceived Son . . .' which leads inevitably to absurd paradoxes and contradictions. Theology at this level is merely playing games with language.

The idea that there must be a creator/creatrix of the universe is also powerfully reinforced by the important device of inventing a word to sum up a process which is very complicated, or a situation which is not properly understood. Since the universe is extremely complex a neat solution to account for its existence is simply to put forward the notion of a creator/creatrix.

This device is known to linguists as 'the hypostatisation of entities'. For example, the process of combustion is rather complicated. Until the nineteenth century it was, however, possible to think about combustion as a process of releasing a 'fiery principle' from combustible substances. This principle was given the name of 'phlogiston'. In fact, however, this entity did not really exist, but was as an invention of the mind, though believers in its existence were prepared to defend their belief with savage valour. Nevertheless, fictions are often necessary tools for thought. We cannot do without them, and they are not dangerous provided they are recognised for what they are – tools for thought, and not things to be revered or worshipped.

Most of us from time to time encounter strange examples of hypostatised entities. I had a friend who was a skilful spinner and weaver. There were days when the quality of her spinning was superior, and days when she felt it was not up to standard. On good days she would say that she could feel the 'power' entering into her. In fact spinning is a rather complex process, and depends for its quality on the nature of the materials and instruments used, and on a nice co-ordination of brain, hand and eye, all of these being subject to atmospheric and other conditions. It is impossible to list all the factors responsible for high quality spinning on a good day. It is much easier to say that you can feel the 'power' entering into you. Nevertheless, it is an example of hypostatisation of entities. Other examples are the Muses, who were believed to touch poets and artists with their finger to transmit their powers, or Luck, the lady who is behind the gambler on a winning streak.

The power does not always seem to come from outside. It can equally well seem to come from within us. Sometimes we appear to have within us a soul or spirit or 'astral body' or other self which can become detached or remain only very lightly attached to our physical bodies. T.E. Lawrence described in *The Seven Pillars of Wisdom* how he had this feeling when riding camels at high speed on long journeys across the desert. By late afternoon he was exhausted by fatigue and heat, but would not rest. Then a time would come when his personality seemed to have left his body and to be flying just above it, looking down on it as if it were an empty shell. I myself have experienced this sensation not from fatigue but from excitement and elation when gliding. From such experiences it would be easy to assume that one had a 'soul' which momentarily left the body and then returned to it again. The real explanation is probably far more complex, perhaps something to do with the computer of one's brain delegating as much as possible to conditioned reflexes and the autonomic nervous system, the rest of one's personality being removed by an act of imagination to a position in which it could hold a watching brief.

Nevertheless, from countless experiences of this type, and for a number of other reasons, the idea has grown up and spread all over the world that people have *souls*. And this is another key feature in the traditional pattern and mould of Western thought. There is, however, little agreement as to their nature. In the West there is a belief that a soul is a single entity. There have, however, been many different theories as to how it came to enter the body – being implanted at one stage or another in the development of the foetus, or existing in a rudimentary form in all living things, and reaching maturity in animals or humans – whereas in China the soul was not thought of as a single entity, but as a compound. If the human body is formed by the combination of two elements, sperm and egg, what more logical than that the soul also should be formed by the combining of two spiritual elements deriving from the Yin forces of Earth, and the Yang forces of Heaven? Or that when the body disintegrates, the soul should also eventually separate out into its original elements, and be returned to its twin sources for recycling? The idea of recycling is, however, abhorrent to many in the West, who regard the soul as an indestructible entity which, though deprived of organs of sensation, is nevertheless capable of experiencing utter joy and exquisite torture.

The idea that the world was made by a creator is, then, the first element, and the indestructibility of the soul is the second which contributes to the Western mould of thought. If the Creator is held to be omnipotent, many problems arise. If not omnipotent, but engaged in battle with evil, it explains why there should be pain, suffering and strife. Neither belief satisfactorily explains why, for example, for a single conception, two million sperm less one are condemned to struggle and die. In the traditional Western mould of thinking the world seems to be a battleground for warring forces – the armies of light against the armies of darkness, the forces of good against the forces of evil. Lip service is paid to the notion of the omnipotent God who 'permits' evil to happen, but in practice the language used, and the concepts that inform the language, are those of warfare – both metaphysical and, all too often, horrifyingly real.

This theory began in Persia about 800 BC with the teaching of Zoroaster, the founder of the religion of the modern Parsees, branched off into Mithraism, the worship of the Sun-God fighting for light against darkness, and reached its fullest development in Manichaeism, which at once time extended its influence from France to China. Even today the rays of the Sun God shine out at coronations in the form of spikes from golden crowns such as were once worn by late Roman emperors. A coronation ritually enlists a monarch as a leader among the armies of light, whether the crown is placed on his head by a Magic priest, a Pontifex Maximus or the Archbishop of Canterbury.

The notion that the world is a battleground, and that 'we' are fighting for the armies of light against empires of evil is vicious and destructive. It has been enthusiastically endorsed for centuries by the Peoples of the Book, convinced that the Lord of Hosts supports their holy wars, or, in the Marxist version, that History is on our side, indicating ultimate victory in the class struggle. The language of the Church Militant here on earth gives continual reinforcement to this militant view of the world. 'Soldiers of Christ, arise!' 'Put on the whole armour of Christ.' 'Onward Christian soldiers!' Today it would be pleaded that this is only a metaphorical way of urging people to get rid of abuses. The Salvation Army, for example, in its weekly *War-cry* never advocated slaughter. But the behaviour of Christian armies has not always been metaphorical, and the use of such metaphors is harmful to scientific thinking. If a cancerous growth needs to be removed from a living body, one does not find the surgeon girding himself with the rubber gloves of righteousness and waging war against the spread of evil. He remains quite clinical. If the world has a future, it will be delivered by those who have steady clinical hands.

Since, in the Western view, the victory of the forces of 'good' over the forces of 'evil' is inevitable, it is important to be on the right side. One must belong to the 'elect', be one of the 'Chosen People'. There was a time when the idea of a Chosen People protected by a tribal God had great survival value for the descendants of Abraham. It helped them to hold together as one people. Later, when established in Palestine, they relied on it as a protective shell to render them unassimilable by their neighbours, in marked contrast to the Chinese whose neighbours were themselves assimilated.

The rigidity of this mould of thought was eased by the early Christians who welcomed into their ranks many people whose customs their Jewish compatriots found most offensive – uncircumcised pig-eaters who enjoyed the nakedness of the human body. To belong to the 'elect' it was necessary to obey the Law, but under the Christians the Law itself was made less rigid. It became possible to say that – pig-eaters or not – what God has made should not be called common or unclean. The broadening of the Law, however, carried with it a mandate to bring within the fold of the elect all those who are not so irredeemably sunk in evil, ignorance or apathy as to be beyond the reach of the Law. It is therefore the duty of the elect to bring them in, like harvesters reaping a ripe field. But the logical end to this mode of thinking is that one is justified in stirring up revolution against the forces of 'evil', in making conversions by force, and, as with the 'Holy Inquisition', in destroying the mortal body to save the immortal soul. Conversion not by example but by force is one of the most unlovely manifestations of the Western thought mould.

Naturally the elect cannot hope to receive divine aid unless they remain within the Law. The *idea of Law* administered by a divine judge, much of whose temporal work is delegated to the princes of the elect, is an essential component of Western thinking. Our literatures teem with references to wise, stern but just judges, to the day of doom, the last day, the day of judgment, to exquisite tortures exquisitely graded for the damned, to advocates, sentences, reprieve, forgiveness and salvation. The peoples of the West seem by nature to be highly litigious, to enjoy a good court case as much as any other drama. But the idea of justice, personified as usual – Blind Justice, impartially holding the scales and sword – is nearer to religion than to science. We even allowed our concept of justice to invade the world of science, starting perhaps with Plato's idea of a just society being like a 'justly' tuned musical instrument, and reaching a climax in the seventeenth century with God the supreme lawgiver giving to the universe Newton's 'laws which never can be broken.' Then came the twentieth century and the discovery that they are not laws at all, but 'statistical regularities.'

So familiar to the peoples of the West is the idea of society under the rule of Law, and under the protection of the almighty Lawgiver, that it is difficult for them to conceive of any alternative. Yet there is an alternative:

> The Tao of Heaven operates mysteriously and secretly . . .
> it follows no definite rules . . .[1]

or again:

> One should not govern by means of punishments and legal pressure, but by looking forth one should exert one's influence (by example) so as to change all things. Spiritual power can no man see. We do not see Heaven command the four seasons, and yet they never swerve from their course.[2]

Perhaps the time has now come for us to bear this alternative in mind, and to think more of laws as crutches for cripples, and of law courts as hospitals for healing, whereas more often they are for the amputation of the limbs of society's casualties. We return to this topic in later chapters.

Belief in a creator god leads remorselessly to the idea that he administers within his Law all that he has created, requiring the elect to fight the good fight against evil, so that their indestructible souls may be judged worthy of eternal bliss after the final victory. This scenario is dramatically exciting. It may be given our enthusiastic approval as drama, but it should not be confused with science.

Developments from the Western idea of the almighty creator as king and lawgiver will, however, first be followed a little further. If one of the great King's subjects breaks the Law, if he is disobedient to God, his offence is given a special name – in English *sin*. And the notion of sin is, it seems, a peculiarly Western concept, another strand in that remarkably resilient pattern of thought that constrains and confines us.

Missionaries have often been hard pressed to find a word to express the idea of sin in the languages of their converts. But in Western Asia, and later in Europe, sin has had a long history. It appears in early times to have been intimately associated with illness. If a person becomes ill, it is, according to primitive reasoning, because he has offended somebody, either a human person, who then used witchcraft against him, or one of the unseen powers. Both sin and illness, according to this reasoning, could be deflected on to animals. The Hebrews had a curious ceremony by which leprosy could be transferred from a person to a bird, which then flew away with it. In Borneo epidemics are transferred onto a model boat which is then floated downstream, bearing the disease away with it. When I once, when travelling by river, reached out to pick such a boat out of the water it caused a great commotion. I was told that if I had touched it, the epidemic would have been concentrated in me. When it was a matter of transferring sin, the Hebrews favoured the goat. The scapegoat bearing away the sins of the people is one example of the usefulness of animals in helping primitive human societies to recover from their self-inflicted psychological wounds. The idea of sin is a clear example of hypostatisation, yet in the course of its evolution it came to be imagined in more and more detail, rather as heraldic beasts and mythical monsters can be classified and illustrated. With the growth of law it became codified, and at the start of the great mercantile age of Western Europe when quantification was the beginning of both modern commerce and modern science, sin also became quantified, so that under the Medici Pope Leo X it became possible to purchase with 'indulgences' remissions of the punishments for the various grades of contraventions. Into such curious byways can the human intellect be led by the misuse of language.

When the idea of a creator god began to develop in the civilisations of Western Asia, such a person not surprisingly acquired many of the characteristics of the all powerful kings to whom the people were accustomed to submit. Such kings were expected to be firm, just, but merciful. They could sometimes be persuaded to be merciful, to make exceptions, or to bend the law a little, but prayers and entreaties would need to be backed up by evidence of sincerity. The clearest evidence of sincerity was, in the early days, an expensive gift, one in which the giving really hurt, a sacrifice as we still express it. The great kings were also very fond of praise. Ordinary mortals were expected to praise the Great King to the best of their ability, and even when he was clearly failing in his duty to protect and preserve his subjects there should be no murmuring or complaint. The idea of democracy was not yet born.

As the mortal monarchs consolidated their power and extended their empires, their courts developed into bureaucracies. Similarly the divine monarchs acquired celestial bureaucracies, to which special duties could be delegated, and from whose members could be expected unceasing praise. This antique attitude still persists, and has perhaps done more than anything else to perpetuate the gulf between the ancient religions and modern science. The gap in thinking between the botanist of today attempting to classify moulds phylogenetically, and Dionysius the Pseudo-Areopagite in the fifth century grading the angels into three classes, higher, middle and lower, each subtending three choirs to praise the Almighty, are separated by more than time, but they are held together by their love of order.

Communal sin could perhaps be deflected with the help of a goat. Personal sin required a more personal effort, some personal sacrifice, ascending over the centuries from material gifts to 'an humble and a contrite heart' offered in Kipling's 'Recessional', to which before long we shall return. In the giving of gifts to spiritual powers, mankind, as always, shows a variety of attitudes. The Greeks in ancient times would wrap up the unwanted bones in fat so that their gods could enjoy a good smokey smell, while the better cuts were reserved for humans. The Chinese in their early centuries realised that there was little point in offering sacrifices to the rhythmic process of the cosmos, but the ancestors with their accumulated wisdom had a better understanding of how these processes should be treated, and it was therefore very worthwhile to offer them magnificent banquets with all the concomitant pleasures, in order to persuade them to come down and help their descendants come to terms with cosmic processes.

But all over the world the most dread and powerful sacrifice of all was that of a man. Human sacrifice was the ultimate proof of sincerity. Much human sacrifice was not to deflect the anger of the gods, but so that the princes of the world after death might continue to enjoy in the spirit world the comforts to which they were accustomed. There was nothing sublime about this type of sacrifice. People along with animals were bludgeoned to death or buried alive so that their spirits could accompany the great lord. What it felt like for the victim comes over very vividly in the ancient Chinese lament translated by Arthur Waley:

> Who went with Duke Mu to the grave?
> Yen-hsi of the clan Tzu-chü,
> Now this Yen-hsi
> Was the pick of all our men;
> But as he drew near the tomb-hole
> His limbs shook with dread.[3]

The story of the proposed sacrifice of Isaac as a lad by his father Abraham rather more than 3,500 years ago is presented as a test of his father's sincerity to his God. When it was found that he was sincere, the human sacrifice could be dispensed with, and an animal substituted, in this case a ram caught in a thicket.

About five hundred years later a similar sacrificial occasion is said to have occurred in Greece. The Greek fleet, about to sail for Troy, was held up by contrary winds. This was because the King Commander Agamemnon had unfortunately shot a taboo animal. The only way in which the cosmic forces could be successfully manipulated was considered to be by sacrificing the King's own daughter. When it was evident that the King was sincere, the offended goddess Artemis relented, and herself substituted a deer.

The essential point in this evolution in human thinking was the realisation that a spiritual change in the giver was more important than the actual gift. Once this was appreciated the idea spread slowly across the world, and animals became accepted as substitutes for men. Then, for reasons of mercy or economy or both, models in wood, clay or paper took the place of sacrificial animals. Today wreaths of flowers on a grave are all that is left of the ancient blood offerings.

But scarcely had the idea of human sacrifice been abandoned in the advanced societies than a new spiritual development took place. This occurred in India where Mahavira, some five hundred years before the birth of Christ, realised that if sincerity is required, the most potent proof of it is when a man of his own accord willingly sacrifices himself for the good of others. Could there be any more potent key for the release of man from sin?

Jain and Buddhist ideas from India slowly made their way westward, sometimes in a fashion that is documented, as when the great king Asoka sent envoys with healing herbs and doctrines to the courts of Antiochus II of Syria and of Ptolemy II of Egypt two and a half centuries before Christ, sometimes by an invisible seepage by sea or along the caravan routes. In such ways did the men of the West receive the idea of self-sacrifice, of monasteries, of hermits, of the rosary and of hell – not the hell they had known till then, a place of murky shadows, swamps and underground rivers, but a place of fire. By the time that Christ was born such ideas were already becoming part of the Palestinian spiritual ferment.[4]

Sin was not the only thing men felt they needed to be released from. Another was *Death.* The place of Death in our patterns of thought – how we explain it, prepare for it, respond to it – is another crucial feature of Western thought. And our views of Death relate directly to our appreciation of Time. A moment arrived in man's evolution when he acquired the concept of linear time. Animals are not bothered by any ideas of time. They live a little in the future, but mostly in the present. Unsophisticated people also live mostly in the present, with a certain amount of their time spent regretting or reliving what is past, but only a little anticipating the future. But at some moment in our history the thought struck home that though we may have the illusion of moving into the future, in fact we are all being sucked backwards at terrifying speed into the past. The past is there like a huge pit, and once in it, what hope is there of ever climbing out? This must have been a far more horrifying thought to people five thousand years ago than is the new realisation which has struck our own generation that our Earth and indeed the whole solar system may be sucked into a Black Hole where the entire world would be compressed to the size of a matchbox, and all the people that ever were could without difficulty dance on the head of a pin! But at least we are spared any real fear, because this prospect does not seem to be immediate, whereas for the people who first obtained the knowledge of linear time, it was the end of their Garden of Eden. Their paradise and primal innocence were lost. Some of the horror that this idea brought with it can still be felt in the old Greek myth of the first great god to emerge from chaos and night – Kronos, Time – who had the repulsive habit of eating his own children even as he still eats us. In the ancient imaginings of our ancestors the two monsters Time and Death are waiting for us in the shadows.

To deal with so grim a situation magic of the highest order was called for. The first step was to break linear time into manageable chunks, such as a year measured by the moon, which is useful for people who rely on moonlight for night-time travelling, or by the sun, which is useful for those who depend on the light and warmth of the sun for growing crops. The next step was to find a way of ensuring that people would be able to get from one time chunk into the next, that is to say, to pass through the death of the old year into the rebirth of the new. We know in detail how this was done in the earliest city states of Mesopotamia, Sumer and Akkad, more than five thousand years ago.[5]

The essence of the magic was to recreate creation by doing it, by drama. There are many different scenarios for the new year drama, but they all have much in common. The Babylonian new year ceremony of Akîtu could be played at the spring equinox or the autumn equinox. Other cultures favoured other dates. The precise date is a matter of convenience. What is important is the act of renewal. In order that there may be renewal it is first necessary to return to the state of primal chaos. For the people of the river civilisations of Mesopotamia, primal chaos was a confusion of flood waters, and creation was the appearance of habitable land above the waters. The original chaotic waters were believed to be under the earth. To restore the original chaos it was necessary to remove the king from his throne, humiliate him, and send him down into hell, the world of chaotic waters, there to struggle with the goddess of watery confusion for twelve days, twelve being the marvellous number which could so easily be divided into useful fractions, and which had given the year its months. During these twelve days a new king, a Lord of Misrule, presided over the world above. Law lost its validity, for the rightful king, the fountainhead of all the laws, had been humiliated and gone. The people were thrown into a state of grief. When the feeling of grief had passed servants lorded it over their masters, children misbehaved towards parents, no limits were placed on eating or drinking, and lovemaking turned into a public orgy, of which the modern Rhineland carnival is but a weak echo.

When the twelve days were over, the king returned from the underworld and celebrated his victory over Death. A goat was driven away, bearing with it the sin, sickness and demons that had plagued the people during the past twelve months. With the departure of the goat the evils of time past ceased to exist. Indeed, the past had been itself annihilated, the world had been recreated, and a new chunk of time had been introduced, bringing with it the hope of everlasting life. It was during the twelve days of chaos, when linear time, like every other orderly thing had been abolished, that the barriers between the past and the present were broken down. Then, as in the long ago tribal days before the discovery of linear time, before man tasted the fruit of the tree of knowledge, the dead who then had never been very far away, but mingled invisibly with the living, came back into the present, alive and in the flesh once more, if they so wished. This mingling of the living and the restored dead took place during the twelve days of misrule, which, in the Christian version, became the twelve days of Christmas, that is to say, the period from Christmas Day to Epiphany. At this time, in the pre-Christian versions of the scenario, there was always the hope that those who came back rejuvenated in body by the blotting out of the past, might be able to live on in the flesh. Such was the ancient promise of eternal life. Such was the refreshing power of water, raising hopes which even today are not entirely extinguished.

Five thousand years ago there was no sharp division between religion and science. The re-enactment of the creation of the world was in line with the most advanced proto-scientific thought. It can scarcely be denied, however, that during the last five thousand years science has made considerable progress, and that the ancient scenario is no longer acceptable as an explanation, though it may be acceptable in other ways. It would probably have died out two thousand years ago under the impact of Greek rationalism, had it not been for events which took place in Judaea. This led to a most powerful reiteration and confirmation of ancient attitudes to the key ideas of Creation, Law, Sin, Time and Death, combining to give a new lease of life to the Bronze Age patterns of thinking.

Any attempt to interpret the early years of Christianity in terms of history leads one into a bog, for even to contemporary observers the facts were far from clear. Much evidence was later suppressed, and attempts were made to iron out obvious contradictions. In later centuries surviving texts were distorted or damaged. Yet round about AD 30 certain events took place decisive for the history of the world. They cannot be ignored if one is to make any sense of today's great issues. Each of us must try to make some pattern of those events which will help us to find a path through the present wilderness.

It is not necessary to describe in detail here the Israelitish form of the ancient scenario, for this has been done elsewhere,[6] but Eliade, after mentioning such aspects as marriages, sexual licence, collective purification through confession of sins and the driving away of the scapegoat, followed by the consecration of the new crops, the enthronement of Jehovah, and the commemoration of his victory over Death, sums it all up with the words: 'But the salient moments remain incontestably the purification of the scapegoat and the re-enacting of the act of the creation of the world by Jehovah.' With the passing of the centuries and the growth of knowledge the antique ritual all over western Asia began to be trimmed of its less acceptable practices, to lose its vitality and begin the long descent into folklore, when quite suddenly it flamed up anew in the person of Christ the King. To understand this it is necessary to appreciate the political background.

Some 1700 years before the birth of Christ, God is said in his wisdom to have given as territory for his chosen people the most bitterly contested area in the world, the point where the civilisations of Asia, Africa and Europe meet and fight, the so-called Holy Land. The armies of Egypt and Assyria crossed and recrossed it. Alexander the Great made it a part of his empire, but when this broke up, it was sucked once again into the deadly contest between the successor states, and into the ideological struggle as to whether the Jews should remain Jewish, or be converted by Hellenism and absorbed into the amalgam of races.

In this time of stress the ancient scenario of order being restored after chaos, and of the redeemer king coming to the salvation of his people, brought new comfort. As Eliade has put it: 'In the understanding of the Hebrew people this cosmogonic victory becomes victory over foreign kings present and to come. Cosmogony justifies messianism and the apocalypse.'[7] The idea of the Messiah, the returning hero marked out for his special role by a holy anointing, grew apace. So also did the intensity of the struggle.

With hindsight we may see this period of history as a 250 year countdown to the sacking of Jerusalem, the turning of the country into a wasteland, the butchery of its inhabitants and the scattering of the survivors around the Mediterranean. It begins with Palestine being torn away from Egypt by Asia, annexed by Antiochus III. The year was 198 BC in our reckoning. This was followed by a nearly thirty year tug of war between rival factions supporting either Greek or Egyptian influence, ended by Antiochus IV making of Jerusalem an 'abomination of desolation'. Then there came forward the heroic Mattathias and his five dedicated sons, and after them some of their sons and wives, to keep the fighting going for another thirty years against those who wished to make them adopt Greek ways. When in the year 134 BC the last leader of the family was killed, their relatives from the Hasmonean branch kept resistance going, often with such success that for a period they were free and self-governing. But one can see how insidious was Greek influence from the way that even this fanatical family adopted Greek names – Alexander, Alexandra, Aristobulus, and so on. Their weakness was that they could not compromise. Having got a measure of independence, that is to say, religious freedom, they fought again for political independence. Having got a precarious political independence, they broke into factions and fought each other. Thoroughly weakened by more than sixty further years of war, feuding and treachery, they then confronted a new and terrible enemy, the Republican armies sent out by the Senate and People of Rome to establish peace and bring back loot. This was done by Pompey, who cracked the defences of Jerusalem and carried out a thorough defiling of the temple, which was rededicated to Jupiter, the high god of the Romans. This was in the year 166 BC. It was, however, still nearly 140 years till blast-off. There was still time to avoid total destruction of the Jewish state.

At this stage in Rome's history, once their armies got into a country they stayed there, draining away money, spreading spiritual contamination, and remaining very still in their fortresses, watching for the first sign of subversion. Nevertheless, it was less trouble to play the game with the help of obedient client kings. Kings could be so corrupted that they offered no threat, and if they allowed their people to get out of hand they could be executed or replaced. A client king who established good relations with Rome, and was clever enough to keep his throne, could, however, do a good deal to soften the harshness of Roman rule. Such a man was Antipater, a petty king from the land of Edom to the south of Judaea, which held the profitable gateway at Petra on the caravan route to Arabia. Such a man also was his son Herod who 'gave the word to slay, and slew the little childer'.

Herod in his early years must have been quite charming. He could talk his way out of anything. He backed the wrong horse twice, once by supporting Brutus and Cassius against Antony in the civil war, and once again by supporting Antony against the future Emperor Augustus. In spite of this he restored good relations and became a welcome personal friend of the ruler of the Roman world.

Herod realised that the one thing which was not advisable in his day was to quarrel with Rome. Under his administration there was a period of peace, and the country began to recover at least sufficiently to enable him to complete a prestige project, the new temple. But to maintain his position in the fanatical and murderous climate of the time was exceedingly difficult. He succeeded by murdering any whom he regarded as a threat, including several members of his own family. He would certainly not have hesitated to 'slay the little childer' if it had seemed worthwhile. He died in the year 4 BC. If that was the year in which Christ was born, he must have acted fast. If, however, Christ was born six years before our conventional year 0, as is now generally accepted, it would have been possible. The chief value of the story, however, is in indicating that in popular belief Jesus was the son of Joseph, who was descended in the twenty-eighth generation from King David, and was therefore of the blood royal. He may be thought of as the Young Pretender of his day, and a threat to the ruling house of Judaea, a house of parvenus, Roman lick-spittles and opportunists at that, of whom Herod, like the late Shah of Iran, was only the second generation to rule. Christ's birth spelt trouble for the authorities. It is not surprising that envoys from neighbouring Parthia (the Wise Men from the East) should have turned up to assess the situation. Any disturbance in Roman controlled territory was good news in Parthia.

Omitting much detail, the next important actor on the darkening stage was Christ, 'the anointed king', himself. He seems to have read the broad political scene in much the same way as Herod. To challenge Rome was futile. But his thinking went much deeper. Let the people pay their taxes, but concentrate on the spiritual life. Love, not politics, was the answer. This was found to be quite unacceptable to all but a handful of his contemporaries. He died. His whole life is now cloaked in the miraculous. Yet the fact that a little boy should have been born in a country across which the 'red-hot iron rake of war' had been dragged again and again for nearly two hundred years – for some eight generations – and should have grown up in that poisonous atmosphere, in comparison with which the atmosphere of Northern Ireland today, or of Lebanon, Afghanistan or Serbia, would seem healthy, that he should have grown up in that atmosphere, and spent his short life speaking of Love, that is in itself a miracle.

Do we really need to argue the realities of the Thirty-nine Articles?

It is worthwhile pausing a moment to consider the conditions under which people lived in Herod's kingdom. Over all was the brooding, vigilant power of Rome, with two main interests – political power and financial profit. The immediate source of power was the Roman governor or procurator, to whom information was fed by spies and informers. A governor was almost invariably tough, having first had the brutalising experience of service in the Roman army. When a country had been conquered the first crop that was taken from it was by way of loot. When the main assets had been stripped, future harvests were assured by putting up for auction the appointments of tax farmers. The man who could offer Rome the highest price got the job. It was then up to him to bleed the taxpayers of as much money as he could get out of them without actually involving Rome in the expense of suppressing a revolt. Such people, backed in their unjust demands by Roman military might, were thoroughly detested. Their moral status was rated only just above that of 'sinners', i.e., prostitutes. Jesus had friends in both these classes – an indication of his moral courage.

In such a society, and after generations of foreign and civil wars, life is extremely competitive, marked by great wealth, corruption and snobbery at the top, and by great poverty, unemployment, sickness and banditry at the bottom. Herod won praise from the property-owning classes by suppressing the prevalent banditry in Galilee for a time. There is no indication that he did anything to eliminate the causes of it. His ruthlessness brought only temporary relief. In addition to all the other sources of tension in that sick society there was the endless bickering and manoeuvring for position of the rival religious sects, the competing claims of alien religions, the struggle for the minds and the money of the ignorant and the uneducated by quacks, magicians and imposters, and – the greatest threat to stability of all – the secret army of 'freedom fighters', the Zealots, who, once they came into the open, could be guaranteed to produce a lightning response from Rome, the thing most dreaded by the Jewish establishment.

There is no quick solution for a society as sick as this. Moral regeneration and the spread of love for another takes time. Even a lifetime is not enough. How then can one ensure that any initial impetus is not lost, but continues generation after generation? Here, surely, the ancient cosmogonic drama could provide the vital continuity, the ancient drama with its promise of cleansing and renewal, but modified to meet the needs of the age, modified once again as it had been so many times before.

Most of the ancient scenario was still perfectly acceptable. Except for the rationalist fringe of Greek society, most people in Judaea still believed in a creator god who had made dry land appear, and who could overcome devils and the forces of evil. The waters of chaos with their power of obliterating time past could still be thought of as 'living water' which gives everlasting life to those who drink it, and whose sins are washed away by submersion in it. The ancient humiliation of the king, his descent into hell, his struggle with death and return to the world he had left, as a redeemer offering remission of sins and resurrection of the body, all these were ancient ideas which had been considered valid since the dawn of cities and the discovery that copper could be fused with tin ushered in the age of bronze. Still acceptable, also, was the belief in the power of the number twelve from its connection with the sun cycle, and with the number three from its connection with the moon cycle, there being three nights of darkness at the end of each lunar month. New ideas more recently evolved in Babylonia included that of the House of the Father in the sky, as opposed to the House of the Mother under the earth. In the Father's House were many 'mansions' or wayside stopping places, in fact twenty-eight 'caravanserai' altogether, where the moon in its erratic annual journey across the sky seemed to pause and rest.

Also of more recent origin was the belief that the redeemer would come in the form of a Messiah to rout the physical enemies of the Chosen People, to judge the living and the dead in a great doomsday judgment, and start a thousand year period of peace, a millenium. Such, and many other ideas, were available at the time when Christ was born, which could be worked together to form a vehicle for carrying forward into the future the paramount ideas of universal love, non-aggression and dedication to a non-material way of life. But there was one great and dread idea which was new to Judaea, and which could completely transform the traditional ritual. As an idea it had been current in Greece for four hundred years, and in India for nearly six, the idea that the most full, perfect and sufficient sacrifice is that of a man – not dragged unwillingly to the tomb-hole as in past ages, but choosing to go, of his own accord on behalf of others. In Euripides' play, *Alcestis*, it is characteristically a woman who chooses to give her life for a man, her husband, and makes her descent into hell in his place, and after a time returns from the dead, thanks to the power of the god Heracles. But in the great cosmogonic scenarios of western Asia, when the king died his ritual death, it was, as in Attic dramas, a form of sacred mummery. Everyone knew that the king did not really die. After so many days he would be back.

When Jesus appointed twelve of his disciples to form a mystic circle, and later warned them of his approaching death, they seemed unable to grasp that it was no symbolic death he was talking about, and least of all the wretched Judas, their trusted treasurer, the only one who spoke in an acceptable southern accent, who seems to have been given the tricky job of making sure that his master was arrested. They continued to plan what they would do, and what posts they would hold, in the new kingdom. But when they saw their leader nailed for sedition, and gasping for breath above them, they were stunned with shock. That sense of shock is with us still.

Meanwhile the countdown continued. Only twenty-eight years now remained before the Romans moved in for the final solution. Only thirty years now remained before Jerusalem would be flattened so that there would not be 'one stone upon another, that shall not be thrown down', as Christ, and no doubt many other clear-seeing people predicted. As the end approached, the turnover of Roman procurators was speeded up, as if two years was as much as one man could stand in that accursed territory. Felix managed to last out eight years, but his successor Festus was in charge only from AD 60 to 62, Albinus from 62 to 64, and Gessius Florus from 64 to 66. These last two distinguished themselves by coming to terms with the assassins, the *sicarii*, who once more swarmed over Galilee, and shared with them the proceeds of their ill-gotten gains. Finally, the Jews could stand it no more, rose in revolt, and were eventually exterminated or scattered.

While this was taking place the Christians, now spreading across the eastern end of the Mediterranean world, took the unfortunate and decisive step of becoming institutionalised,[8] in spite of their founder's suggestion that they should be invisible as salt, which nevertheless gives food its savour, or as unstructured as yeast, which nevertheless leavens the whole loaf. Quite excessive attention was paid to the antique vehicle with which they were to propel their founder's ideas into the future, and far too little to the diffusing of the belief in the power of love and the possibility of non-aggression, on which the future safety of the whole world would depend. One gets some idea of this imbalance on reading the various creeds which were formulated for party members as check lists of their orthodoxy. They make no mention of belief in the power of love.

One aspect of this development was the struggle which grew up between Christianity and the last strongholds of the scientists in Alexandria. The end of that struggle has been described by Carl Sagan,[9] in a few tense lines:

> The last scientist who worked in the Library was a mathematician, astronomer, physicist and the head of the Neoplatonic school of philosophy – an extraordinary range of accomplishments for any individual in any age. Her name was Hypatia. She was born in Alexandria in 370 . . . The growing Christian Church was consolidating its power and attempting to eradicate pagan influence and culture. Hypatia stood at the epicentre of these mighty social forces. Cyril, the Archbishop of Alexandria, despised her because of her close friendship with the Roman governor, and because she was a symbol of learning and science, which were largely identified by the early Church with paganism. In great personal danger, she continued to teach and publish, until in the year 415, on her way to work she was set upon by a fanatical mob of Cyril's parishioners. They dragged her from her chariot, tore off her clothes, and armed with abalone shells, flayed her flesh from her bones. Her remains were burned, her works obliterated, her name forgotten. Cyril was made a saint.

The story of Hypatia has often been told before, and can easily be sentimentally exploited. One needs to be careful about blaming the people involved. The upper crust of educated society in the Roman world was interested in science for its own sake, not in the moral questions raised by science. The same is partly true of our own society as regards the people who wield power and who decide to which branches of science their nation's resources will be channelled. Few of them are interested in the morality of international science, but rather in how it can be used to strengthen their own nation state against the others.

The established Churches, on the other hand, have yet to come to terms with modern cosmology – essential for their survival.

Two points stand out in this early Christian story from which we should take warning. One is aggressiveness. The other is the power of institutions. Before they were organised into powerful communities the early Christians don't seem to have been particularly aggressive. In fact a fairly impartial observer remarked, 'Behold these Christians, how they love one another!' But once people begin to love institutions more than each other aggressiveness follows.

Aggressiveness is by no means limited to any one part of the world or group of its inhabitants, but it has been peculiarly developed by the Peoples of the Book. Judaism, the religion of those who first worshipped Jehovah, Lord God of Hosts, Mighty in Battle, set the tone and infected the rest. Exulting in their conquests of lesser tribes and nations, they showed an implacable loathing for those by whom, in the game of power politics, they had been treated with relative generosity. As Psalm 137 puts it:

> O daughter of Babylon , . . . happy shall he be that taketh and dasheth thy little ones against the stones.

Such vicious sentiments are inconceivable in the gentler Buddhist and Taoist worlds.

In due course those who drew the sword perished by the sword, and the remnant were scattered. After nearly two thousand years of insecurity and suffering enough of them came together again in 1948 to form a new nation. One would have thought that they of all people, having recaptured their ancestral homeland by the sword, would be generous in victory, determined to see justice done to the weak and homeless, and to renounce aggressiveness for ever. Far from it. The Lord God of Hosts is with them still, and those who are not of the Chosen must pay the price. Jewish history may be taken by the rest of the world as a warning against the danger of getting locked in on a self-image which is bound to cause an endless repeating of what has gone before – aggression, reaction, oppression, revolt, diaspora, round after dreary round, each time with sinister variations.

When Christianity budded off from Judaism there seemed to be a chance that the syndrome would be broken. A new Book evolved, inspired by the example of the Prince of Peace, in which individuals and nations would not demand an eye for an eye and a tooth for a tooth, but would turn the other cheek even when suffering aggression themselves. Eventually the meek might inherit the earth.

Unfortunately the mould of Western thinking was too strong, and could not be broken. The aggressive pattern continued. The new Christian Church, like other minority movements set on evangelisation, needed an enemy to help them concentrate their energies. The first enemy was their own people, those Jews who did not share their new enthusiasm. The Christian Church then went out of its way to make life difficult for the Jews for the next nineteen centuries. Only very recently have there been any signs of repentance.

When the Jews were scattered, following the destruction of Jerusalem in AD 70, and no longer presented a concentrated opposition, the early Christians split into different groups, and attacked each other, gnostics against the Church of Rome, the Church of Rome against the Church of Constantinople, (the 'Orthodox'), and each of these against countless heresies, and both of them against any other religion.

It is obvious that a scenario which has its roots in the Bronze Age and even earlier cannot fail to be ambiguous and wide open to different interpretations, none of which can be tested as could a scenario based on modern science. Different interpretations developed thick and fast, the most virulent heresies coming from Britain and the Slav countries, provinces under the Roman Empire which had never been slow in backing rival emperors. The doctrine of original sin, for example, depended on the belief that the human race was descended from Adam and Eve. If it can be shown that there is no scientific basis for this story, a great deal of rationalisation is needed to keep the doctrine in being, as was attempted. But even in the days when Rome was falling to the barbarians, this improbable theory was under attack, and it required all the energy and eloquence of St Germanus to keep the Britons on the narrow road to salvation. As early as the year AD 200 Origen was speculating that souls could turn into demons trapped in human bodies, and was putting forward the rather modern idea that creation is eternal and not a sudden and finite act. A century later the Arians were denying the divinity of Christ, while in the fifth century the Nestorians maintained that there were two Christ persons, one human and one divine. In the third century the Persian Manes developed the theory of the dual origin and existence of good and evil as coexisting principles, which led men to think of the world as the kingdom of evil, an idea which took firm root among the Albigensian and associated heretics. Against these poor people the Church, through the ministrations of the Dominican order, carried threatenings and slaughter with a zeal that would have delighted St Paul in his unenlightened days. In the twelfth century 20,000 heretics were butchered in Béziers alone. And about the same time the Church turned its attention eastward again. The Prince of Peace put on the armour of righteousness and went crusading against the Infidel. The Saracens, who were preserving what was left of Hypatia's scientific civilisation, were inevitably regarded as the forces of evil, comparable to the 'evil empire' of recent American thinking. The mould of Western thought is still unbroken.

The fact that Islam was also a fighting religion and offered a quick route to paradise for those who died in its holy wars, spreading the faith, meant that Christianity had a worthy adversary. The challenge was not refused, and by the time the

Crusades were over, and the Moorish kings ejected from Spain, the Christians had little to learn about intolerance and fanaticism. There were, in fact, fresh fields for its deployment. Unblessed by their gods with horse or gun, the peoples and empires of the Americas collapsed under the hammer blows of the cross.

But the old Islamic enemy remained, no longer Arab, but seen as more terrible in the form of the Turks. A long established and benign civilisation should have made the Turks Greek, as Greek civilisation had previously Hellenised the Romans, and as China absorbed the Turkic, Mongol and Manchu invaders of that country. But this did not take place. The Turks absorbed what was left of the Roman civilisation and made it their own, so that today even the Roman bath is referred to as a Turkish bath. How far the West had strayed from the universal love of Christ is illustrated by the action of Pope Callixtus III who, in 1456, prayed that all the evils for mankind of which Halley's comet gave clear warning, might be diverted from the Christians and concentrated on the Turks!

The memory of all-conquering and wide-ruling Rome was, however, not yet dead, and in due course the British, well-educated in a thoroughly misleading literature which had the militant histories of the Jews and Romans as its foundation, soon identified themselves as the Lord's Chosen People and established the Pax Britannica to replace the Pax Romana. In mid-Imperial career Britain produced a very strange poet – Rudyard Kipling. Had he been born seventy-five years later, and entered his prime in the swinging sixties of the twentieth century, we could picture him wearing jeans and carrying his guitar to the places he did in fact frequent – the world's slums, factories and lumber camps. Being a man of an earlier age, however, he visited such places rather conventionally dressed, and because of his dress and accent, was readily mistaken by the British ruling classes for one of their own. The astonishing result was that he became known as a 'Singer of Empire'. When, in the high noon of British naval power, the fleet was to be reviewed at Spithead, he blazoned his 'Recessional' in the pages of *The Times*, where those members of the ruling classes who were in the habit of reading could scarcely miss it. An apothecary sugars the pill, and Shakespeare would get the attention of the groundlings at the start of the play by bawdy jokes or the flash of swords. Kipling got the attention of his readers by opening his 'Recessional' with lines they would find thoroughly acceptable:

> God of our fathers, known of old,
> Lord of our far-flung battle-line,
> Beneath whose awful Hand we hold
> Dominion over palm and pine -
> Lord God of Hosts, be with us yet,
> Lest we forget – lest we forget!

As the poem went on, it became less and less acceptable –

> Still stands Thine ancient sacrifice,
> An humble and a contrite heart . . .

> Lo, all our pomp of yesterday
> Is one with Nineveh and Tyre!

> If, drunk with sight of power we loose
> Wild tongues that have not Thee in awe . . .

> For heathen heart that puts her trust
> In reeking tube and iron shard,
> All valiant dust that builds on dust,
> And guarding, calls not Thee to guard,
> For frantic boast and foolish word –
> Thy mercy on Thy People, Lord!

Although some got the message, many read it as confirmation of Britain's right to rule, provided of course that they continued to 'do the decent thing'. In retrospect it is clear that, so far from spurring them on, the 'Singer of Empire' was trying to rein the sahibs back. Kipling, himself, due to his classical education, could scarcely visualise an alternative to the British Empire, unless it were another Empire run on worse lines. The idea of the Chosen People was indelibly printed on his mind, but though he was unable to break the mould completely, he chipped it a little, by regarding as the Chosen People all those of any class or race who were 'within the Law'. But his was an unusual and oddly misunderstood voice.

We repeat: Once people working together in small groups allow themselves to be structured into a large institution, they are on the road to power, and thereafter to corruption. Even ecumenism, which at first looks so attractive, ultimately means greater power, and thereafter greater corruption. The scenario adopted by Christ unfortunately lent itself very readily to the building up of hierarchical power, for it derived historically from the ideas of the kingly states of western Asia. Illustrating the curious love-hate relationship which so often occurs between colonies and their political masters, the Christians modelled their growing institution as a mirror-image of the detested political beast of Rome. Once power had been achieved it was not long before a detached Roman would have been able to observe, 'Behold these Christians, how they butcher one another.'

There is no need to recapitulate the recurring horrors, but one must stress that people with genuine doubts and misgivings were persecuted for holding to the 'wrong' ideas. A wrong idea is not only one which does not fit into a system, but one which endangers an institution. The poor peasant Cathars, for example, who lived in the eastern Pyrenees, in trying to establish a purer life endangered the institution of the Catholic Church. Part of their heresy was that they found it impossible to believe that the bread and wine of the sacraments are turned into the body and blood of Christ, for they reasoned in their earthy way that if this were true, their own vile bodies would soon be excreting the body and blood of their Blessed Lord through their impure human organs.[10] In a science-oriented society it is considered an advantage to have people who hold different views on theories. That is the essential difference between a theory-oriented society and one which is faith-oriented.

If an institution is authoritarian it is only a matter of time before it comes to be policed. Much has been said against the Inquisition, but often for the wrong reasons. The real damage was not done in the upper echelons when thinkers like Galileo were silenced, or like Giordano Bruno were burnt at the stake, for such people were often of the quality, usually well-connected, or having property and therefore deserving consideration. The men who directed the Inquisition were intellectuals who were concerned with broad issues such as political instability. They were the top of the ants' nest.

Below them, proliferating in a myriad unseen channels, was the army of spies, bully boys and thugs, who are the nauseous by-product of any police state. If a scientist insisted, after being warned, in publishing his book, he knew the price and was prepared to pay it. But the price which poor peasants and ordinary people had to pay was the poisoning of their lives and of their communities by suspicion and fear. An informer had great power. With the breath of fear on his side he need only whisper to a man that he could save himself much trouble by parting with his money, or to a woman that she could avoid further enquiries by inviting him to her bed. The genius of Spain found a new use for the Inquisition by directing its activities against Jews, as if they too were heretics, and against the poor defeated people of the great empires of South America. Today it is easy to forget that the Inquisition was not abolished until 1835. Named by some ecclesiastical humorist 'The Holy Office' its descendant still lives on in Rome under the seemingly innocuous name of 'The Sacred Congregation for the Doctrine of the Faith', like some malignant seed awaiting the passing of the rationalist water, and the return of a new spring of faith.

The greatest danger of all for the Peoples of the Book is an excessive reverence for scripture. Such reverence exists not only in western Asia and Europe, but throughout the world including some socialist countries where until recently the writings of Marx and the later prophets played a corresponding role. In India also there has from ancient times been a deep veneration for the Vedas, and among the Sikhs for their more recent holy writings. In extreme form this attitude becomes fundamentalist, and the possibility of a clash between the world's rival fundamentalists, none of them with minds open to the arguments of others, but locked in bibliolatry, is horrific. Fundamentalist powers each armed with nuclear warheads and a Messiah should effectively shorten human history. In healthy contrast are the mocking writings of the Taoists, who warn their readers that a truth once written is a truth lost, and that though books cannot be avoided they should not be trusted! Neither reverence nor scepticism can be taken as guides. The Tao like a river knows its way to the sea. The would-be navigator needs neither oar nor sail.

REFERENCE NOTES

Chapter 3.

1. *Huai Nan Tzu*, ch. 9, trans. Needham (1954), Vol.2, p.561.
2. From the commentary of Wang Pi (ca. AD 240) on *The Book of Changes* cited in Needham (1954) Vol.2, pp. 561–2.
3. Trans. Arthur Waley, (1934), p.311.
4. Needham writing of the development of 'ethical polarisation' has classified the whole world-wide gamut of heavens

and hells in *Science and Civilisation in China,* Vol. 5, pt 2. p.77 ff. tracing its source to Iranian dualism.

5. See Eliade, (1949) ch.2, 'La régénération du temps'.
6. Eliade, *op. cit.* p.99.
7. *Ibid.*
8. As W.H. Auden put it:

   'The Christians saw their hopes decline
   To a late lunch with Constantine.'
9. Sagan, (1980) p.335-6.
10. For the life and beliefs of Cathar peasants in the early fourteenth century see Ladurie, (1980).

4

A Place for Reverence

Reverence and scepticism are two different attitudes, but they are not incompatible in the same person; they apply to different modes of thought and behaviour. Scepticism is often essential, though in many activities it is inappropriate. The pleasure of opera, for example, is lost if one is sceptical about the plot. In cosmology, on the other hand, traditional beliefs about the origin of the world, no matter how venerable the books in which they have been preserved, are no substitute for rational analysis. A scientist may be filled with wonder at the beauty or complexity or magnitude of the universe, and yet be highly sceptical of some theoretical explanations of what is observed. The great pleasure of the early Taoist books is that they combine these two modes – wonder and reverence for all that is – with humorous scepticism about human behaviour and its justifications.

Scepticism is lulled by ritual reading of the word, and words often repeated become an incantation. Insistence on incantation is then made the means by which Holy Books are defended, since once they begin to be argued about and contradictions become apparent, they may cease to cohere. The oneness is lost for all but fanatics as the two-and-seventy jarring sects tear them to pieces. As soon as the New Testament is read in the critical spirit in which one should read a newspaper it is found to teem with contradictions, omissions, signs of suppressed evidence and interpolations of a later date. To take one example, there is the matter of money, and the alleged weakness for it of Judas Iscariot.

If a person wishes to found a new movement, three things are necessary – charisma, organisation and money. Without charisma he will not rise above the individuals with a message who address crowds at Speaker's Corner or in market places. With charisma he will attract others and persuade them to join him. When others join him, if there is much work to do, if 'the fields are white unto harvest', the work must be shared out, with specialisation of function. This requires organisation. If the work is heavy and long, it will require full-time service. People who work for an organisation full time usually need to be paid if they and their families are to be fed. This requires money. The nucleus of Christ's infant organisation consisted of at least thirteen people as full-time workers, some of them married and with dependants.[1] How much did it cost, and where did the money come from?

In late twentieth century terms Judas, the treasurer, would scarcely have been administering the equivalent of less than £100,000 per annum. No doubt many of the contributions were gifts in kind, but these had an exchange value, and often food had to be bought, rooms at inns to be rented, clothes and shoes to be repaired or renewed. Every movement has its expenses. The treasurer of an organisation of thirteen or more full-time workers would, if he were dishonest and astute, have plenty of opportunity to make something for himself on the side. But if that is so, it would be very much in his interest that the organisation should remain in being. The thing he would most fear would be the death of the charismatic leader on whom they all depended. While he lived funds would continue to flow in. What possible reason could there be for him to wish to kill the goose that lays the golden egg?

The theory that Judas was a thief is not only implausible but implies that Christ was a bad judge of character, and chose for the most responsible post in his organisation someone who was unreliable. The traditional version of these events can give no better explanation than to say that Satan entered into Judas, which implies that up to that time he had been honest. This explanation is so unconvincing that countless attempts have been made to find an alternative. Every reader must fend for himself. If Judas was a crook, why did he sell his master so cheap? Why only thirty pieces of silver? This was the basic price for an ordinary slave, or a workman's wage for a month. A higher quality slave with secretarial training would cost much more. The value of a slave in the ancient world may be roughly equated with that of a family car today.[2] When Judas accepted his thirty pieces of silver he was certainly not being offered the equivalent of a quality car. In the world of spies and double agents what traitor would sell the head of his organisation to the enemy for a price only a little above that of a clapped-out old banger?

But perhaps there is another explanation. Perhaps the priests didn't need his information. Perhaps his information was of little real value, but they paid him a nominal sum to retain his goodwill. This seems likely, for Jerusalem was full of spies and informers, and there would be no difficulty in having the Nazarenes with their giveaway dialect followed. Nazarenes would have had as much chance of hiding from the authorities in a garden on the Mount of Olives at a time of mounting tension, let alone after causing an uproar in the Temple[3], as would a pop group visiting London have of concealing themselves in Hyde Park after smashing the windows of Westminster Abbey.

It is difficult to avoid the impression that power politics is just below the surface. In fact this is made very clear by the writer of

St John's Gospel, who reports that at a council of Pharisees the point was made that if they allowed Jesus to carry on exciting the people and raising the political temperature, 'the Romans shall come and take away both our place and our nation.' The chief priest, Caiaphas, then continued, 'It is expedient for us, that one man should die for the people, and that the whole nation perish not.[4] In other words if the country was to enjoy even limited independence under the Romans they had to demonstrate that they were not prepared to tolerate any sort of subversion or nationalist uprising.

From that moment onwards, therefore, there was a similarity of intentions, but a difficulty in putting them into practice. The Jewish authorities wished to make an example of Jesus to demonstrate their good faith to the Romans, and Jesus apparently intended to make of himself a voluntary sacrifice in such a way that his message would never be forgotten, but be burnt into the minds of men by the horror of it, generating the power for the mystery whose celebration would propel his ideas into the future. But the Jewish authorities, whose law, after all, was subordinate to the law of Rome, were only likely to get the Romans to agree to an execution if it could be shown that the accused was an insurrectionist and a danger to Rome, whereas Jesus' message stressed non-violence and pacifism. With such a programme it was difficult under Roman law to be found guilty. Jesus seems to have found a solution to the problem by going through the motions of preparing an insurrection, but with minimal military equipment, ('two swords are enough'), and stressing the supernatural reinforcements which he could expect, ('forty legions of angels'). But at the last moment, when the populace was keyed up for revolt, he deliberately refused to fight, and let himself be made prisoner after only token resistance by the impetuous Peter. This left the Jewish authorities in an awkward position. They could scarcely release him without loss of face, but they had a poor case for securing an execution.

Very ingeniously they played on the weak spot in the Roman administrative system, which was the suspicion felt at headquarters in Rome for the men in the provinces who held any sort of power. All that was needed was a little crowd manipulation, with threats to denounce the Governor to the higher authority in Rome for tolerating sedition. That settled it.

Thoughts such as these may pass through the mind of the attentive churchgoer as he listens to the readings from the Bible. I have merely written here the explanation of those long past events which has eventually seemed to me a possible one. But I realise that there are perhaps a good many hundred other explanations of those troubled years of history, and that many people will find my interpretation quite unsatisfactory. Those who are members of authoritarian churches with fixed views have no problem. Others like myself may find it difficult to accept traditional views without questioning them. Everyman may well be perplexed. If he reads commentaries, studies the sources, allows himself to give some credibility to the newly recovered views and traditions of the rival sects in the early Christian Church, and hears the discussions of theologians and Biblical scholars, he will be overwhelmed by the uncertainty of things. If certainty is what he is looking for he will look in vain.

> Myself when young did eagerly frequent
> Doctor and saint, and heard great argument
> About it and about, but evermore
> Came out by the same door as in I went.

The thought then strikes home that perhaps the historical accuracy of these events is not really so important. It may be interesting to know whether Jesus really had brothers, or who was wrapped in the Turin shroud, but is it important? Even today, with all the means we have for recording events, it is often quite impossible to find out the reasons why people do things. It would have been even harder in first century Judaea. Even at the time when it happened there were uncertainties and different versions of events. It was said, for example, that Judas hanged himself in a fit of remorse[5], but also that he threw himself down from some eminence, or rather 'fell headlong' with the astonishing alleged result that 'he burst asunder in the midst, and all his bowels gushed out.'[6] This is something which doesn't happen to people even when thrown out of aeroplanes, on account of the strong muscle wall holding their bowels in. Was there foul play, or did he attempt some sort of Japanese-style suicide? To try to answer such questions today, and to piece together the fragments of evidence is a fascinating study, but it is irrelevant to the world's future.

Concentration on historical facts, and savage disputing about the form and functioning of the vehicle which had been assembled to carry into the future the ideas of universal love, non-aggressivity and a renouncing of material interests in order to foster the life of the spirit, distracted attention from its precious cargo. Once the men in the movement had succeeded in getting all-male control of it, and had started out on the long and repugnant road which led to the subjection of women – for a man 'is the image and glory of God: but the woman is the glory of the man . . . neither was the man created for the woman; but the woman for the man.'[7] – once women were in subjection there was little to hold men back from their usual games of empire building and the glorification of institutions. Once they were in a position to demand love for the institution and loyalty to those who ran it, universal love flew out of the window. Looking back on the last two thousand years of religious experience in Europe we must admit that it has probably done more harm than good, yet its failures have been redeemed by the lives of many individuals in whom love blossomed in spite of the environment in which they lived, and often in defiance of the institution to which they were expected to give their loyalty.

The first need is to encourage sensitivity to that which inspires our feelings of reverence and awe, and yet to temper them with wide-ranging scepticism, and, as familiarity breeds affection, to allow our love for all that is, to grow. It is interesting that the idea of universal love first seems to have developed among the artisans and working classes rather than with the well-educated or the wealthy. It was first preached in China between the years 479 and 381 before Christ, by Mo Ti, who was apparently a wheelwright living at almost the same time as that marble polisher with a questioning mind – Socrates. The idea of universal love may have developed in many different places spontaneously. Four hundred years after Mo Ti it was preached by the carpenter of Nazareth. Direct diffusion or not, the climate of opinion is all the time being affected by subtle changes and exchanges in different parts of the world. Whereas technologies have until quite recently been diffused rather slowly, ideas not dependent on a mechanical process or instrument seem to have got about relatively quickly. That makes sense. If an idea could be conveyed by telling a story while sitting round a camp fire on the great caravan routes, it would travel as fast as men can walk. If, on the other hand, it was necessary to set up a workshop and demonstrate it before it could be believed, the acceptance of a new idea might be delayed for years.

As an example of this one may see how slowly the idea of making paper travelled. Though so useful an invention, and so badly needed, it took fourteen centuries to get from China to England.[8] By way of contrast we may notice how the new art of thinking in paradoxes, if it did not spread from one centre to another, developed in rapid succession first in Greece with Zeno of Elea, about the year 450 BC, then in China with Hui Shih only about 130 years later, about 320 BC, and still later in India with Nagarjuna in the second century after Christ. As an example, Zeno wrote: 'The arrow in flight is at rest.' Hui Shih expressed a comparable paradox in the words, 'There are times when a flying arrow is neither in motion nor at rest.' The idea of universal love could well have been conveyed by stories told round camp fires on the caravan routes.

Universal love, as Mo Ti understood it, does not seem to have been a very inspiring concept. Perhaps it was rather like the modern notion of the solidarity of the working class. But at least it broke with the feudal idea that one's love and loyalty should be reserved for one's family, clan or liege lord. It represents an important step on the road towards love of one's 'neighbour'. About a hundred years earlier the idea of love had been widened by Confucius when he said that within the four seas all men are brothers, though the men he was thinking of were perhaps educated men and men of good family who followed the same ethical code. Toward the common people he would have felt protective but not loving.[9] Even earlier one reads in the Bible, (*Leviticus* 19:18) the injunction probably composed in the seventh century BC 'to love your neighbour as yourself'. But neighbours at that time did not include foreigners. The Israelitish people were being advised not to quarrel with each other, but to hold firm against the menace of aliens.

The great step forward was taken when philosophers realised from the existence of paradoxes that spatial and temporal divisions end in contradiction, that things are interrelated, that all is one. When a person thinks of all as one, his attitude to love must change. Hui Shih expressed it in the words: 'Let your love spread to all the myriad things; heaven and earth count as one unit.'[10] When love spreads to all the myriad things, one's neighbour is included among them.

At this point it may be helpful to apply modern thought processes to the idea of love. Today we no longer seek for the essences of ideas which correspond to single words, but feel more at home when ideas are stretched out on a measurable scale or pinned by their nodal points to a graph, or when we detect an evolutionary trend from lower to higher stages, or from simple to complex. So let it be with 'love'.

While Mo Ti in China was urging his belief in universal love, Empedocles was at the same time working out a theory in Sicily that all things had come into being as the result of love and strife, or as we would say now, attraction and repulsion, or concentration and dispersal, or contraction and expansion. But this sort of behaviour belongs to particles and to the atomic and subatomic world. It is not appropriate to use the word love at this level of organisation.

It is still not appropriate to use it when speaking of organisms which grow or multiply by assimilation or division, when that which is absorbed becomes part of the absorber, or when the parts after division become separate entities, as when some unfortunate starfish, torn in half, becomes two starfishes. The beginning of the ladder of love is to be found in those creatures which have evolved to the point at which they have developed specialised sex organs.

From this point on begins the marvellous biological story in which the creature with male characteristics becomes excited by what he senses is going on around him to the point at which he casts his seed upon the waters, whereupon some of the creatures with female characteristics which happen to be near him will, if they are lucky, get their eggs impregnated. With them, as with us, huge numbers of seeds are swept away downstream, and get assimilated into the life cycle once again, but as food. For the future the evolutionary trend is not to reduce the losses in spent seed, which will be recycled anyway, but to make sure that at least one in every million is on target and fertilises an egg. We may follow the process up the evolutionary ladder, and see the gun which fires the volleys of seed getting closer and closer to the target, until the two creatures concerned actually embrace; nor can we fail to admire the splendid economy by which the male who has performed his act of service to the female then becomes her nuptial meal. Mating at this stage seems to be a chance affair. The female gives the signals by winking lights or by odours borne on the wind, but it doesn't much matter who turns up, so long as it is an active male. If they arrive in their dozens that is all to the good, as when frogs gather in what looks like an orgy. But such a meeting is no orgy. Frogs are serious people, and they have a job to do. Encounters at this level may be regarded as forming the lowest rung on the ladder of love, or, if we change the metaphor, the fertile soil from which the tree of love will grow.

At the second stage mating is no longer haphazard. Competition introduces an element of discrimination and choice. If the female has the choice, the rival males must woo her. Now begins the marvellous pageant of courtship and display. There are many things that can be displayed – courage, strength, agility, beauty, radiant health and even possessions. All these are factors which are still of interest to human couples, but humans have added a few more such as humour and intelligence. There is, however, one other factor which may be observed in certain animals, and especially in courting birds, which is of importance, and that is concern for the partner. It would perhaps be a false interpretation of observed instinctual behaviour to suggest that birds show affectionate concern for their mates, but they certainly show concern, evolved in response to the pressures of the lives they lead, as a way of ensuring the lives of their offspring. A female likes a male who shows concern. By selection, generation after generation, its importance has increased. Concern is heightened and blossoms as affection. It becomes one of the most important elements in the complex alchemy of love.

Together with the growth of affection for the desired partner goes growing selfishness and increased rivalry towards competitors. Other forms of affection such as love between brothers can be disrupted, so great is its power. Fathers occasionally become the rivals of their sons, and friends become enemies. Now begins the agony of love, the agonies of hope and despair, of love which is not returned, of temporary and of permanent separations, and all the passion and pathos of people in this condition which is transmuted into literature.

A child's first awakening is when, at about the age of seven, he begins to get an idea of the immense size of the world and of space outside it, and of the immense tracts of time going back and back, when things have been happening which he knows nothing about, but can now begin to discover. Then in his teens comes the second great awakening, when young people suddenly discover that there is more to their senses than they had been aware of, and every sense is heightened by its vividness and delicacy. Now not only flowers and foods but bodies have perfumes which speak a new language. Colours are richer and are seen to be in countless combinations and varieties. Human voices are found to possess new subtleties of timbre and intonation, and the memory of a single syllable spoken by the loved person evokes their entire being and personality. The fingertips also discover a new kingdom, the world of texture, with smoothness of skin, silkiness or roughness of hair, the hard and the soft, the hot and the cold, the wet and the dry. All nature opens up and blossoms, world on world, and world within world, permutating and proliferating for ever, and then suddenly combined and concentrated in the instant of love. This is the golden fruit which must most urgently be plucked, even if the price to be paid is banishment for ever from the innocent garden.

It is not surprising that almost every young person feels the plucking of this fruit to be a matter of the most urgent importance, for we have behind us a history of nearly 400,000 generations of people, at first ape-like and then human, who have been selecting each other as mates because they shared this same response. There is nothing more beautiful than the bloom on the faces of people who have plucked the fruit and are happy together. Like every bloom it fades and withers with the anxieties of having children or of not having them. This can be accepted, for waxing and waning is the Tao of life, and the Tao embraces failure as well as success, but in their hour they did not lack the spirit to pluck the golden fruit.

Until recently many gifted people were confronted with a difficult choice. Being married almost certainly meant having a family. Having a family almost certainly meant distraction from their life's work, for which total dedication and concentration of energy were essential. Until recently money could buy servants and a certain relief from the investment of energy which children require, or if the gifted person was a man, he could push the burden onto women. But we may well ask how many plays Shakespeare would have written if his Anne had followed him to London, had there borne him half a dozen brothers and sisters for Susannah, Judith and Hamnet, and had insisted on his taking his share in nappy washing and in getting up at night when the children were crying.

Mankind is on the eve of achieving complete control of the art of reproduction. In theory a few test tubes of frozen sperm will be enough to keep the human race going for centuries. From the point of view of reproduction a large male population has become an anachronism. Gone are all the old fears that haunted primitive men that fertility might cease if their women did not walk past a certain magical rock during the waxing of the moon, or if people did not hold promiscuity carnivals, and then punish themselves during Lent, or if they did not observe taboos concerning the right time for intercourse, or the right people to have it with. In the not very distant future it will be possible for the entire human race to be reproduced as a clinical operation, if that is what we want. Already our morals are in a state of flux. The whole world has become a giant pot in which the temperature is steadily rising. Whether it will turn out to be a crucible from which will be poured the alloy to make a wonderful deep-toned bell, or a cauldron from which will be ladled some witch's brew, remains to be seen. It might seem that the choice is between turning the whole world into a giant laboratory, or else into a garden of love inhabited by flower people. But that is, perhaps, not the choice, for love and science are not incompatible.

Laboratory reproduction is only one factor that has altered our thinking. In the past a woman was regarded as property, subservient, physically weaker, responsible for the fertility of a married couple, associate of the powers of darkness, and the custodian of a great deal of Bronze Age rubbish. All this is being swept away by the new machines which are completely indifferent as to the sex of the person who operates them. One may visualise a world in which women have the same autonomy as men, in which reproduction is in the hands of the laboratory technician, and in which those who require pleasure can have it artificially induced by electrodes stimulating the appropriate areas of the brain. Yet human beings have been given an astonishing talent for making love. Is this talent to be buried in a napkin and forgotten?

It is worth pausing a moment to consider the nature of this talent. Unlike other animals, men and women are able to make love all the year round. In the display of courtship finery they can outdo even the birds. Animals prefer to mate in a particular place, the modest elephant privately in the forest, dogs publicly in the centre of a barking chorus. Man as a species is happy to make love in solitary couples or in groups, in darkness or in daylight, on land, in, on or under the water or even in the air. Animals mate in one position only. Man, the inquisitive and inventive animal, has found ways of making love in countless permutations of position.

The subject is hedged around with taboos and fraught with racial and religious, not to mention physical differences between the various branches of the human race, but the medieval Taoists believed that each posture had specific therapeutic qualities conducive to long life and good health, and these may have been included as possibilities worth trying.

Unlike the animals men and women come together in many different moods. The mating bull approaches the waiting cow with serious intent, quite without humour. It takes a human to extract humour from these antics, as when, in the days before the cinema, Sicilian children were assembled of an afternoon to enjoy the hilarious coupling of a jack and jenny ass, as if they were comedians on a stage, whereas English children in rural areas, similarly starved of entertainment, would meet in the butcher's yard to watch the grim drama of pigs having their throats cut. Nor was horror or humour restricted to the observation of animals. Groups of people in Asia and Africa in colonial days were diverted in their leisure by impressionistic sketches of how the white man boss would clumsily attempt to pleasure his wife on a Sunday afternoon. What provoked their humour was the lack of grace which caused Africans, for whom every movement is rhythmic, to describe Western ballroom dancing as 'doing geometry with their feet.'

The mood of lovemaking in the human species can be urgent, serious, reflective, languid, tender, inquisitive, scientific, jocular or hilarious. A sign of maturity in people is when they discover that reverence and humour are not incompatible. This was wonderfully illustrated by the Athenians of the great generation in the days of Pericles, who, at the dramatic festival in honour of the god Dionysus, could show the god himself on the stage as a victim of mistaken identity, being given a hilarious spanking. Yet this same god was portrayed in the tragedy of Euripides, *The Bacchae*, as the terrible intoxicating power of the mind when uncontrolled by rational thought. That which was feared, loved and worshipped could also be laughed at. Love, too, is an intoxicating power which needs to be laughed at. It is entirely healthy, therefore, that it should be thought of not only as a primitive power to be feared, but as an aspect of nature that commands our reverence, and also as a subject for fun. From this point of view one can enjoy the humour of the erotic game described in *The Perfumed Garden* of Shaykh Nefzawi, in which a woman lies on a bed balancing aloft on the sole of her foot a lighted oil lamp, which her lover does his best to upset by his assiduous attentions.[11]

In lovemaking that which is beautiful, or graceful, or even just interesting can wake in us a mood of reverence, while that which is crudely mechanistic provokes our hilarity or contempt. The first seven to ten years of adulthood are an age of exploration. Those who do not explore then are likely to want to explore later when it is more difficult. Some young people are hemmed in and tethered by their parents or the institutions they belong to so effectively that they do not discover this world until very late. But those who discover it in their youth explore it to the limits of their capacity and then, the seam being apparently exhausted, adjust by diverting their energies in other directions, or by making a reassessment of their situation.

Those who make a reassessment may be saddened by the passing of the bloom of youth; such sadness indicates a failure to identify with the Tao of things; or they may believe that they made a mistake in the choice of person to live with, and that this can be put right by pairing with somebody else. Sometimes a wiser choice is made the second time, but very often the pattern is repeated, for the choice is largely dictated by the unconscious chemistry of our bodies. Some people marry and remarry again and again, stuck on the same rung of the ladder, always hoping to meet the ideal partner who does not actually exist.

The next step up the ladder is, however, again dictated by our animal past. Those gene packages which have survived as reproductive machines in the form of efficient animals have not been worried by morals. Sensitive humans have been worrying about morals for several thousand years, but the genes carry on regardless. There are certain laws which cannot be broken. 'Do not breed at all and you suffer genetic extinction.' 'If you overbreed you will exceed the food supply and must pay the penalty.' 'Scatter your seed widely and you have a better chance that some offspring will survive, but, on the other hand, invest work and energy in bringing up children, and those best looked after will have a better chance of survival.' It is only very recently that new developments in science have begun to make it possible for us to get control of our genes, and to direct human evolution in the way in which we think it should go.[12] Nevertheless, we carry with us from the remote past two contradictory tendencies, one towards monogamy for the better caring of our offspring, and the other towards promiscuity which, in earlier times, by widening the scatter, increased the chances of at least some survivors. Enter the 'Seven Year Itch.'

The itch for variety led in the past to much injustice. Men with sufficient strength, power or wealth would gather as many women as they could manage into a harem, in the manner of their ancestral forest apes. The women so gathered in large harems led ineffective and lonely lives, often seeing no man except a eunuch from one year to the next. But since in most populations men and women are roughly in balance, the fact that the rich and powerful had forty or fifty or more wives meant that poor men could often not afford or obtain even one. To overcome this imbalance, and to cope with the itch for variety, prostitution was invented or came into being as a way of overcoming an artificial woman shortage. Once again women were the chief sufferers. The profession seems to have come into existence at the very beginning of urban civilisation, when the building of walled towns and private houses made of stone or brick, which could be defended like fortresses, made possible the amassing of private wealth. Prostitution is unlikely to disappear until the conditions which caused it also disappear.

The itch for variety in sexual experience has also been satisfied by what Catullus called 'furtivos amores'. In agricultural communities from China to Peru, where work was hard and entertainment scarce, undercover lovemaking provided an antidote to boredom for the whole community, as well as a form of sport for the participants. In ancient Rome it must have been a very exciting and dangerous sport, for the jealous husband was justified in law in killing on the spot the couple he caught outraging his honour. More often, however, there was a live and let live code of tolerance, similar to that which prevailed at the court of King Louis XV. Today there is a new development of quite open wife-swapping. This, however, often ends up as the same group of people living as newly assorted couples, still on the same rung of the ladder of love.

On the third rung of the ladder selfishness weakens and competitiveness is no longer important. It is now a matter of widening experience, of sharing that experience, and of early blooming of compassionate love for people who in brasher days might not even have been noticed, or who would have seemed unattractive. The Tao now begins to display its infinite diversity: the range of people who are always unlucky, the people who continually knock things over, people who are often ill, whose bodies are curiously shaped or different from the norm, people with weird interests and hobbies – such people now start tumbling into the net of compassionate love. As one climbs the ladder of love the animal in us weakens and spiritual affection grows strong. People who never got a footing on the second rung can sometimes by spiritual strength pull themselves up onto the third. At this level there is no sense of possession. One exists for the other person or people. 'In the kingdom of heaven there is neither marriage nor giving in marriage.'

It is not possible to reach the fourth rung of the ladder without strong spiritual affection, for at this level people are welcomed in, even though bad-tempered, vindictive, savage, boring, ugly, or with repulsive habits. Yet their need is great. It is easy to invite to love's feast those who are beautiful, gentle, kind, amusing, powerful or rich. Yet we were counselled long ago to go out into the highways and byways and bring in to the feast the destitute and the afflicted. This means that they must be accepted as they are. There was no rider to the parable that before they can be admitted to the banqueting chamber they must pass a test in good manners, in intelligent conversation, that they must have a medical certificate showing they have no communicable diseases, that they have been deloused, given a good bath, and no longer smell. This is the level of love at which saints begin to operate, as when Saint Catherine of Siena, feeling revulsion from the wounds she was tending, is said to have bitterly reproached herself. Sound hygiene was incompatible with charity, so she deliberately drank off a bowl of pus.[13] More in keeping with modern thinking are the countless Mother Teresas who spend their lives helping those who live in 'poverty hunger and dirt'. At this fourth level of love the storms of sexual passion have died away, or have been transformed into a golden shower which falls upon the unjust and the just, the lovely and the unlovely, without fear or favour.

At the fifth level the horizon widens still further, for it is no longer a matter of feeling compassionate love for humans only, but all living things now fall into the net in which nothing may be called common or unclean. The seeds of this potential affection may be noticed, not yet generalised, but reserved for particular creatures, among children who love pet mice or snakes or spiders and other such animals as are not much favoured by adults. Yet this is the love which led St Francis to refer to the lice which feed on human bodies as 'celestial pearls'. It is also the love which forms the moral of Coleridge's poem 'The Rime of the Ancient Mariner', for after the ancient mariner has shot the albatross, the ship is becalmed, day after day; one by one his companions die of thirst, and still the ship is becalmed, till,

> The very deep did rot: O Christ!
> That ever this should be!
> Yea, slimy things did crawl with legs
> Upon the slimy sea.

Then, at last, after much suffering,

> A spring of love gushed from my heart,
> And I blessed them unaware.

It was only after this act of love that sweet rain fell.

One of the saddest things is to see love falter and die. But it is only at the second level of love that this happens. At the third level love never falters. It has an internal strength. At the fourth level it begins to develop an unquenchable radiance. At the fifth level, if you are so fortunate, you are part of the universal radiance.

There is no clear-cut border between animal and plant or between things organic and inorganic. Nor is it clear where love blends into a feeling of association or assimilation. Although a person may say he loves mountains, the word has been stretched by metaphor, and means that walking in mountains or looking at mountains gives him pleasure, but the pleasure given by inorganic things is quite different from that which arises when love is a mutual exchange. Somewhere love blends into a feeling of identification with what Taoists call 'the myriad things'. Once we understand the scale of the myriad things we can find our place in it, and identify with the whole, become part of the One. The scale of the myriad things can then be thought of as existing at three levels. In identifying with things at each level our feelings are different. At the level of the immensely great, as when we consider the volume and the heat of the Sun, the enormous distances to the nearest other suns, the size of our galaxy and the vast number of galaxies so far observed, the quantity of matter in space, and its gravitational force culminating sometimes in Black Holes, all the things which Pascal found so mute and terrifying, our feeling should not, if we have learnt to identify, be of terror, but of awe.

At the other extreme, the supremely minute, we allow ourselves with the help of microscopes or of imagination to descend down and down to the level where we seem to be walking through a bushy undergrowth, that which clothes the body of a bee, or observing, like a city seen from the air, the circulatory system of a creature too small to be detected by the naked eye.

Falling still further we enter into the voids inhabited by racing particles. Our feeling then towards things so much smaller than ourselves is that of wonder. It is only in the regions where things are roughly of our own size and more or less manageable, that a fitting reverence blossoms with love and humour.

Modern man's mastery of technology has blighted reverence. Our machines roar round the harvest fields sucking in everything in their path, grain, ears, stalks, weeds, insects and small animals; they are beaten and blown this way and that, sorted, rejected or stored, and the air outside is filled with a trailing cloud of dust. The man who drives the combine harvester all day drives on and on thinking of straight lines and turnings. How different when it was reaped armful by armful with a sickle, or earlier still, ear by ear with a flint knife, so that the reaper was aware of the individual differences between one ear and the next, between corn in this part of the field and that, and the very slowness of the work made it possible for him to identify as he passed all the idle weeds that grew there, and the creatures that lived in his sustaining corn, so that in some measure in the course of his arduous work he was able to identify with the myriad things himself.

This identification was expressed in the ceremonies at the end of harvest, of which we still have a wan survival in the decoration of churches at harvest festival. What has changed is not necessarily the attitude to the spirit of the cornfield, but our attitude to co-operative work, and our attitude to that which is produced. Corn is no longer a blessing but a dividend resulting from an investment.

Similarly our attitude has changed to the animals we kill. People at a primitive level of technology realise that we must all eat and be eaten. To sustain life in a hunting economy, men kill animals, but they do it with reverence, and an understanding of mutual interdependence. This is not true, however, of those who have moved out of the hunting economy but not yet progressed very far up the ladder of modern thinking, and kill their beasts with mindless savagery. But the squalid butcheries of modern man are an affront to the myriad things, and an invitation to retribution by the Tao, for the Tao is not mocked. Even the bread we eat is sliced with the cold steel, not broken reverently with the hands. When eating we allow ourselves no time for the pleasures of touch or smell, and often only for the crudest of tastes, while we read an ephemeral newspaper before hurrying out. The Fast Food Bar is the Temple of Anti-Reverence.

Of course there can be no reversal of technology, but it is still possible for us to regain our lost sense of reverence toward the myriad things. This requires not a new religion in the old sense, for there can never again be religions of the Bronze-Age pattern. Science has made it impossible to go back unless civilisation collapses and the Stone Age returns. It requires not a new religion, but a new attitude and way of life. How can such a change be brought about? What is the way out of the wilderness?

There would seem to be four courses of action. The first is to ignore the numinous and identify with machines, adopting their standards of speed, economy and efficiency. The more like machines mankind becomes the more we shall find a machine environment tolerable. Many might try to cling to the old numinous way of life, seeing it shrinking year by year, rather as the poor Bushmen have seen their rich spiritual life of paintings and holy places shrunk to a routine of visits to desperate water holes. If the main body of mankind abandons the numinous, those who do not will become the Bushmen of the future. It may be that the machine people will prove to be the fittest to survive, and that controlling so much power will induce in them that awe which underlies the numinous. But if mankind possesses a talent for the numinous both Testament and Tao urge that it should not be ignored, for the way of the Tao is to explore every possible path and permutation, while the servant who buries his talent has little hope of reward.

The second way would require drastic modifications to be made in all the religions of The Book, for if they are out of harmony with modern science they cannot be very convincing. The old religions have naturally been evolving and undergoing modifications century by century since they began, but the sudden and rapid development of modern science during the last few hundred years has put them under great pressure to evolve with comparable rapidity. But whereas people approve of the rapid development of science, they disapprove of rapid changes in religious beliefs which are meant to provide permanence in a shifting world. The 'liberal bishops' are therefore likely to have their work cut out in getting their flocks to follow them along the knife edge trails that lead to better pastures in the centuries ahead. One must not grumble if there is a good deal of fudging on the way, for one of the functions of speech is to make unpalatable ideas acceptable. For example, the ancient Father-God of primitive times has long ago been metamorphosed into God the Father, but now the Father is himself under fire as a concept capable of explaining the origin of the world. In public debate I have heard Christian apologists say that 'God the Father' is simply a metaphorical way of describing the creative spirit in nature. But this is fudging the issue with words, for what is meant by spirit? If by spirit one means something that is able and willing to alter the laws of nature in answer to prayer, the gulf between religion and science is as great as ever. Another verbal device which might be helpful in an age of transition could be borrowed from Hinduism, by transposing God is Love into Love is God.

For centuries yet the world is likely to be divided between those who believe that changes can be effected by prayer and those who do not. Nor can it be tested, for it would be felt that prayers said in order to test a theory scientifically are not valid or acceptable prayers. What is important is that the issues which divide us should not be fought over. The world's flock must nose their way gingerly over the precipitous passes, allowing time for those who are weak and timid to decide in whose steps they will tread.

There is a third way, which is to regard the numinous attitude to life as a mode of perception. Our appreciation whether of deity or Tao comes to us by many paths. For the mathematician there is a beauty in numbers and elegant equations; for the scientist there is wonder and awe in the immensity and diversity of the forms of matter; for the musician and artist there is the exaltation of the spirit which accompanies the refinement of the senses through art; for those whose lives are spent in care for their families or of other people's children, identification with the Tao, or with God's work as some might put it, is no less possible. But many the world over express their identification through rituals which are in effect ancient drama, the *doing* of what is believed to have happened. But the numinous spell is only effective if accompanied by real belief in the effectiveness of what is done. Hence the insistence on faith. If there is a contradiction between the facts of science and the articles of faith the drama will collapse. Once the essential verities are disentangled from scientific contradictions, it is perfectly acceptable for the numinous mode of perception to be expressed through a Bronze Age scenario. The fact that the scenario may include angels, devils, saints, immortals, sages, dragons, cloud-scaling ladders, heavens, hells, joys and torments need not invalidate the drama. Our appreciation for the numinous in Aeschylus' *Oresteia* is not invalidated by the fact that the Furies, the Eumenides, have no place in modern science or psychology.

The fourth course of action is more decisive. If it is found that the vehicle on which the precious cargo is being carried into the future is beginning to break down, the cargo can be transferred to another vehicle, or alternatively the vehicle can be given a fresh lease of life by borrowing spare parts from another one, to repair it. This is by no means impossible. It was done in Britain in the first century, when the great druidic system of belief and education, with its fine infrastructure of teacher training colleges and its ancient oral literature no longer met the spiritual needs of the age. All this was placed at the disposal of newborn Christianity, making Britain the first Christian province in the Roman Empire. A new vitality was then engendered resulting in the Celtic Church, highly decentralised and free of any cravings for empire-building such as overtook the Church of Rome. On the contrary the benign leaven spread unobtrusively through the now barbarised western provinces and on into the lands which had never been under Rome's rule. Irish and British monks brought them light and learning from the last corner of the Western Empire where Greek, the language of science, continued to be read and taught. Today Taoism offers a comparable chance of revitalisation, a chance to reconstruct our ancient Bronze-Age vehicles on modern lines, so that they may carry our aspirations for universal love, non-aggressivity and renouncing of material interests far into the future, and not be abandoned a few centuries hence as museum relics of primitive thinking. For many the surgery involved will be too painful. Many will be convinced that such a possibility should not even be considered. To them I would say, 'I beseech you in the bowels of Christ, think it possible that you may be mistaken.'

REFERENCE NOTES

Chapter 4.

1. That Peter was married in clear from *Mark* 1: 29–31 which refers to Peter's mother-in-law. I am grateful to Mrs Dorothy Gallagher of Ditchburn Place, Cambridge, for drawing my attention to this passage.
2. On various currencies and values of coins used in Judaea, Syria and neighbouring countries, see Millard, (1990), pp. 72–3 and 91.
3. It should be noted that though *Matthew* (21:12–13), *Mark* (11:15–17), and *Luke* (19:45) all place this incident shortly before Jesus' arrest and execution, *John* (2:13–16) places it some years earlier. This is an example of the sort of contradictions referred to in the second paragraph of this chapter.
4. *John*, 11:48.
5. *Matthew*, 27:5.
6. *Acts*, 1:18.
7. *1 Corinthians*, 11:7–9.
8. See Carter (1925) p.95 on 'Paper's Thousand Year Journey from China to Europe'.
9. In the *Lun-Yü* (12:22) Confucius says: 'Do not do to others what you would not wish them to do to you.'
10. The *Kuan Tzu* also expresses a similar idea: 'If you consider yourself as part of the great One, you must love the Myriad things as you love yourself.'
11. See Burton (1982), p.148.
12. The dangers of this became obvious in the early application of Nazi eugenics. See however Dawkins (1976), p.203 ff. 'Memes: the new replicators'.
13. Mary Douglas (1966), p.7.

5

Power and the Way

Mankind today is at a still quite primitive level in the handling of political power. We still raise our hackles like fighting cocks to warn others off our rights or territories. This may be seen in the behaviour of heads of state. They arrive in a foreign country and are led off to inspect a guard of honour. This is a ceremonial way of saying 'Kindly note that we are not defenceless.' Many nation states reinforce the idea of nationality by having a national day when dense columns of troops strut and swagger their way down the main avenues of the capital city. In the days of muskets this was bad enough. It is more threatening now because soldiers are technicians, masters of weapons that can wipe out a crowd in a matter of minutes. Even more sinister is the introduction after the row on row of jackbooted men drilled in the chilling performance of the goosestep, of vehicles drawing guns capable of demolishing large buildings, and of intercontinental missiles able to wipe out entire populations. Such parades can be taken as indicators of the level to which a nation has risen out of barbarism, or the level of decivilisation to which it has sunk.

Once the incubus of military braggadoccio has fastened on a nation it is difficult to get rid of. One way, however, is to allow such ceremonies to become antiquated, and even endearingly ridiculous. In Britain, for example, the beloved monarch is escorted on important occasions in an antiquated golden coach pulled by horses, and guarded by anachronistic cavalry. Such demonstrations pose no threat. Many countries have found non-military alternatives. In China, for example, national days are celebrated with garden parties rather than with military parades.

Nation states, a political form which developed in Western Europe out of feudalism some six centuries ago, have spread right across the world. They came into being as the result of a particular mode of thinking which can be derived not only from the city states of ancient Greece, but from the religions and philosophies which came out of ancient Persia, then as now called Iran. It will certainly be some centuries before we have outgrown them.

A mode of thinking which has characterised the western half of the Eurasian landmass for over three thousand years came out of ancient Iran as one form of dualism, by which things are seen in contrastive pairs. It is a common practice the world over to group opposites in pairs – black and white, day and night, hot and cold, good and bad, male and female. Yet few of them are divided by a clean cut. Most of them are end points on a scale. Black shades into white through a range of greys. Day turns into night through an intermediate twilight. Even male and female are distinguished by varying degrees of masculinity and femininity according to an individual's body chemistry. Unfortunately for the human race the ancient Iranian dualists included in the contrast a moral judgement. Good and bad were among their pairs of opposites. With good they classed such ideas as day, light, hot, strong and male. To these they opposed night, dark, cold, weak and female, which were bad. The whole attitude was expressed in religious terms. Their supreme god, Ahura-Mazda, was the principle of good, and in perpetual conflict with the principle of evil, Ahriman, later to be personified as the Devil.

This form of thinking reached its most extreme form in Manichaeism, the religion founded by the Persian Mani, who was not only crucified by his enemies, but stripped of his skin as well.

Once this mode of thought is adopted, it colours all one's actions. Life becomes a battle in which an individual likes to think he is on the side of the good, the true, the right and the just against the bad, the false, the wrong and the unjust. Victory for the good is inevitable. No sacrifice in so just a cause is too great. The world is now littered with war memorials commemorating the 'supreme sacrifice' of the victims of this gigantic philosophic error. Yet it is not without poetic appeal. It makes good drama. In time its infection spread into Judaism, Christianity and Islam in the West, and made some progress in the Buddhist lands of the East, including China. But in China, mercifully for the planet, it arrived too late to affect the growth during its vital formative years of an alternative mode of thought. This alternative is expressed in Taoism and was present in Confucianism. It will be considered shortly.

Ancient Iranian dualism had four malignant effects. First, it led the faithful to believe that total victory over the forces of evil was not only just, but possible and ultimately inevitable. Life was, therefore, thought of as a battle in which the enemy were evil and the war glorious. From this it is but a short step to the second malignant effect, the general glorification of war. War in the days when this philosophy was formulated was conducted by kings against rival kings. It is not surprising, therefore, that whole religions were organised in the service of heavenly kings, and that the religious activities of populations were mobilised to aid in the prosecution of their heavenly wars. The third malignant effect was, therefore, the organisation of religions on a monarchical basis. As men were dominant in these monarchical societies, and as, according to this form of dualism, women belonged to that set of the pairs which included the dark, the cold and the evil, it is not surprising that women were regarded as instruments of evil who could only be prevented from inflicting much harm on society if men kept them firmly in check. The fourth malignant effect of ancient Iranian dualism was, therefore, the subjection of women, a state of affairs which still has a long way to go before it can be fully corrected.

This form of dualistic thinking spread across the lands conquered by Alexander the Great, and then through the Roman Empire into Western Europe. From there it was carried to the Americas, Africa and Australasia. Wherever it took root and spread it became natural to think in contrastive pairs – sheep and goats, saints and sinners, Democrat and Republican, Conservative and Labour, and to expect or demand loyalty to one or the other. 'Away with all trimmers.' 'A man cannot serve two masters.' Although cases may occur when things need to be divided by the clean cut rather than along the scale, division into contrasting pairs is often unjustified and damaging. There are countries where sheep and goats are so similar that they can hardly be distinguished, and others where school teachers and university lecturers can hardly live at all unless they serve two masters, that is to say, hold down two or more jobs in different institutions.

For people who have been brought up in dualist environments and believe in a Creator of the world who also created mankind, it seems quite natural that He should have created the male first, and the woman later in a subservient capacity. Of all the myths which have befuddled human thinking during the formative centuries, the story of Adam and Eve in the Garden of Eden is hard to beat. In many parts of the world there were folk memories of an earlier time before the scramble for personal possessions, when people followed an innocent and carefree life.[1]

The people who lived in Mesopotamia also had such memories, but with a difference. They seem to have located their ancestral home somewhere near the source of the two rivers, the

Tigris and the Euphrates, for these were two of the four rivers which were said to flow out of the Garden of Eden. A characteristic of such stories is that men and women walked about naked, a perfectly natural thing to do in a temperate climate, and fed themselves on the earth's abundance. The garden, however, belonged to its creator. He was the original landowner who liked to inspect his property from time to time, and keep an eye on the tenants. What landowners cannot stand is for the tenants to have ideas above their station. After Adam and Eve became acquainted with the serpent of wisdom it became obvious that they were getting too clever by half, and the landowner felt he had no choice but to evict them. They were therefore driven off his property and left to shift for themselves, something which must have happened many a time to the unfortunate peasants of this early civilisation. But the story was shaped in such a way as to make it clear that these feckless people had brought all their troubles on their own heads. Adam was held entirely to blame, and naturally he passed the blame on to his woman, Eve. The moral of the story would seem to be – 'Always do as you are told; pay no attention to what women say; keep your station, and don't try to find out about things which don't concern you.'

With the story of the Garden of Eden we may compare one from China about an idyllic place called Northendland, or 'Ultimate North', which was believed to be as remote from China as Ultima Thule was from Rome. Like the Garden of Eden it had four rivers running out of it, but in other ways it resembled the island valley of Avilion – 'where falls no rain, nor hail, nor any snow, nor ever wind blows loudly'. The Chinese story goes like this:

> There was neither wind nor rain there, neither frost nor dew . . . In the midst of it there was a mountain called Amphora, shaped like a vase, at the top of which there was an opening, in the form of a round ring, called

> Hydraulica, because streams of water came out of it continually. This was called The Divine Spring. The perfume of the water was more delicious than that of orchids or spices, and its bouquet was better than that of wine or musk. The spring divided into four rivers which flowed down from the mountain and watered the whole land. The climate was mild, there were no poisonous emanations causing sickness. The people were gentle, following Nature without wrangling or strife; their hearts were soft and their bodies delicate; arrogance and envy were far from them. Old and young lived pleasantly together, and there were no princes nor lords. Men and women wandered freely about in company; marriage plans and betrothals were unknown. Living on the banks of rivers, they neither ploughed nor harvested, and since the *chhi* [emanation] of the earth was warm, they had no need of woven stuffs with which to clothe themselves. Not till the age of a hundred did they die, and disease and premature death were unknown. Thus they lived in joy and bliss, having no private property; in goodness and happiness, having no decay and old age, no sadness or bitterness. Particularly they loved music. Taking each other by the hand, they danced and sang in chorus, and even at night the singing ended not. . . . King Mu of Chou, when he was on his journey to the north, also found this country, and forgot his kingdom entirely for three years.[2]

It is good to know that such countries exist for those who can find them. But to get there thc traveller must abandon many prejudices and conventions. As in the kingdom of heaven there is neither marriage nor giving in marriage, nor is there any need for nakedness to be covered by the deceit of clothes. It is a country inherited by the meek, where all are sustained by living water, without competition, envy or strife. No miracle is needed to change this water into wine, for the water of life is wine, the wine of the Sufis of which Jalalludin Rumi wrote:

> Before garden, vine or grape were in the world
> Our soul was drunken with immortal wine.[3]

No angels with flaming swords guard this country to keep outsiders away, but all who survive the travails of travel are welcomed in, like beggars from the highways and byways invited to the great king's feast. We are now wandering into mystical country. But before we start that journey there is much thinking to be done.

By great good fortune an alternative philosophy had grown up and reached maturity in China before ancient Iranian dualism, with its belief in incessant struggle ended only by victory, moved in to blight and corrupt. This alternative was the early form of Taoism, in which struggling for power was considered the highest folly, and the great precept inscribed above the dragon throne of the emperors of China was: *Wu wei. Wu wei* means 'not interfering with the processes of nature', or more positively, 'using the natural flow of events'. Literally it means 'Not do' or 'without doing', and in the past was wrongly translated as 'do nothing' and 'take no action'. But this misrepresents the idea. 'Taking no action contrary to nature' is certainly not to be taken as a recommendation to sit down and do nothing, resigning oneself to fate. On the contrary, a small expenditure of energy at the right time, and in the right way, brings big returns. We are vaguely aware that there is a tide in the affairs of men which should be taken at the flood, and that crossing the bar at low tide can lead to damage. But life is so complex that it is difficult to visualise how the principle of *wu wei* can really be applied. Let us take an example, and see how *wu wei* operates.

Every great city has a pattern of traffic circulation. To cross a city from north to south or from east to west requires an understanding of its pattern if this is to be done quickly and smoothly. The pattern includes a convention that vehicles travel in some countries on the right of the road, and in others on the left. If this convention is not understood the motorist wishing to cross the city will soon be in difficulties. There are, however, certain streets where the traffic flows only one way. If the motorist struggles against this convention he will be in even greater difficulties. If he doesn't oppose the oncoming traffic when he meets it, he will find himself forced off his route into a time wasting detour, whereas if he had known in advance which streets were one-way, he would have been able to take advantage of smooth circulation.

There are also, even in modern life, signs and portents which we must be able to read and understand. If, for example, the motorist sees a constellation of three coloured lights set at the intersections of streets, he must learn to read their message. Suppose he sees a green light replaced by a yellow one, this he should take as a warning that he should not continue on his journey until the omens improve. A solitary yellow light is certain to be followed by a red one, and the red is a most evil portent. Under no circumstances should he continue on his way. Red, however, considered in the West to be the colour of fire and danger, will eventually yield to the fresh green of spring, when the ice breaks and everything begins to move again. When it shows, the cars begin to flow once more through the city's arteries. Green, in the Tao of cities, is a very good omen, and when he sees it the motorist can respond by pressing on his accelerator. Omens can, of course, be misread, or the system may break down, causing snarl-ups in the city's traffic circulation. But on the whole, being mechanical, such signs can usually be depended on in helping to decide one's course of action.

Omens which are non-mechanical are not so reliable or so easy to interpret. A minister, for example, who serves a powerful king or dictator, will observe his ruler's face with the same close attention as a motorist gives to traffic lights, particularly on occasions when he is feeding in information. If, in the course of doing this, he notices that the ruler's face suddenly becomes red, this is a very bad omen. It probably means that the ruler has become extremely angry, and is a signal that warns of danger ahead. A sudden change to white may also indicate anger, or perhaps fear, or may indicate sickness. Face signals were a subject of intense study in ancient China, were worked into a system, and are used in a conventional form in plays to indicate character on the faces of actors, and hence their likely actions in Chinese drama even today. Because the world is so vast and complex, no signals for interpreting the Tao of things should be ignored, but they need rethinking and testing with the methods of modern experimental science. It is difficult, for example, to feel much confidence in the warnings of astrologers when, in the West, they regard the planet Venus as the planet of love, whereas in China the same planet is regarded as the planet of War, disease and death! On the other hand it already seems clear that sunspots give regular warning of atmospheric changes on the earth, which may result in changes of weather. This in turn may affect the growth and harvesting of crops, and as a result food supply, human health, and ultimately perhaps economic stress and even war.

Let us return to the Tao of traffic problems, and the simpler world of cities. Cities are partly man-made and partly natural. Nature provides the terrain for a city, its hills, its marshes, its water supply, perhaps a river, and perhaps a place where the river can be forded. Man supplies most of the rest, but this too is shaped by nature. What the houses are made of depends on what materials are provided by nature. How the houses are built depends on the climate and possible dangers to be guarded against, and so on. In early cities people followed the Tao very closely. To begin with they had to live near their water supply. As ancient Rome grew, improved technology made this unnecessary. Aqueducts brought in water sufficient for five million people. When the aqueducts broke down and could no longer be repaired, the population shrank, as once again the inhabitants had to live near their water supply, the river Tiber.

People who live in or near great cities learn a great deal about the Tao of cities, just as those who live or work on ships learn about the Tao of winds and currents. A city dweller learns that there is an inward tide of people from say 0800 to 1000 hours in the morning, and an outward flow in the evening from say 1700 to 1900 hours. These tides are known as rush hours. A motorist who has studied the Tao of his city, and in fact any type of traveller into the city, will, if it can be arranged, time his journey so that he arrives just before or just after these rush hours. If that is not possible he may yet be able to learn what are the points of greatest congestion, and find ways round them. If he belongs to an appropriate organisation he may be able to use short-wave radio, and profit from the advice of other people with more knowledge of the situation then he has himself. Such action may be regarded as participating in a form of group consciousness, but this group consciousness is at a purely mechanical level. To interpret the Tao of a wider world a higher form of group consciousness may be called for. People with this ability are still, in the early childhood of the human race, very rare. In Taoist terms they are known as *sheng jên*, sages, *chên jên*, true men, or *hsien*, immortals.

In cities, therefore, the would-be sage studies the inherent patterns of things and adapts to them. He rapidly learns that brute power alone does not help. A huge juggernaut lorry may have the size and power to force its way across the city in defiance of conventions and traffic patterns, but it will not get across more quickly than a driver in a small car who knows all the back streets. If the world may be thought of as one vast city, it is clear that it contains a number of super-powered juggernauts, a number of flashy and expensive cars whose owners think they should have priority, and a huge number of pedestrians struggling to go this way and that, and clogging the streets. This chaotic state of affairs will not be remedied by doubling the size of the police force, or by looking for inspired guidance to one Redeemer Sage. The situation will improve when whole populations begin to study the Tao of things, recognise the tides and patterns, and make small changes each in his own living circle, to promote the ethos of the Tao by abandoning force, and foregoing private advantage.

Taoism treats the use of force at two levels – force used by an individual, and force used by the State. The problem of power and the use of force in attack and defence had become a vital matter for statesmen in China during the three centuries from 480 to 221 BC. This turbulent period was known as the time of the Warring States. Equilibrium had been upset by four new inventions: money; the cross-bow; stirrups for cavalry charges, and the smelting of iron. They threw society into a ferment right across the ancient Eurasian continent. In the West this period saw the rise of the Greek city states at one end of the time bracket, and the defeat of the Carthaginians by the Romans at the other. Somewhere in the middle of the period one of the early Taoist books was written. It is usually referred to as the book of *Lao Tzu*, the work of Master Lao, but is also known as the *Tao Tê Ching*, the Classic of the Way and of Power. As with the Gospels, many of the sayings are no longer clear, and though attributed to one person, are evidently derived from various sources. As with the Gospels the discovery of these sources, or of earlier versions of the text throws new light on the early meaning. In December 1973 Chinese archaeologists excavated a tomb at Ma Wang Tui in Honan, and found two versions of the *Tao Tê Ching* written on silk, and at least five centuries older than the oldest previously known text. Quotations made hereafter from the *Tao Tê Ching* will be based on these early versions.

What the *Tao Tê Ching* has to say about war is decisive:

> Through compassion, I can triumph in war and be impregnable in defence. When heaven sets up something, it keeps it, as it were, behind ramparts of compassion.[4]
>
> There is no disaster greater than being without an equal. Being without an equal nearly cost me my treasure. [The author speaks as an experienced statesman.] Thus when the two sides raising arms against each other are evenly matched, it is the one that is sorrow-stricken that wins.[5]

Without going further back than World War Two it will be recalled that the side which entered the fighting with the greatest reluctance was eventually victorious. This does not mean to say that no aggressive war is ever successful. Both sides can make mistakes. Nor, in dangerous times, should a state, according to Taoist thinking, be defenceless, but:

> Arms are instruments of ill-omen. When one has no alternative but to use them, it is best to do so without relish. One should not glorify them. If one glorifies them this is to exult in the killing of men . . . When men are killed in great numbers, one should look on them with sorrow. When one is victorious in war, this calls for the observance of funeral rites.[6]

War making, in the *Tao Tê Ching*, is spoken of as something requiring clinical detachment. 'One who is good at fighting is never roused in anger.'[7] The commander 'should be resolute but must not be arrogant; he should be resolute but must not brag about it.'[8] A clinical commander is likely to make the best decisions, but once battle is joined it is often too late to prevent commanders prosecuting their business with relish. One recalls stories of Churchill making clinical decisions with his chiefs of staff on the use of bombing, but adding at the end when cautioning them – 'Business before pleasure, gentlemen, business before pleasure.' He could not forego relish.

The *Tao Tê Ching* in its military thinking was centuries ahead of its time. Until the nineteenth century a gentleman in the West was expected to defend his honour by recourse to arms. The *Tao Tê Ching* simply states: 'Arms are not the instruments of the gentleman.'[9] Wars were known to be followed by depopulation and famines. 'Over the place where troops have encamped brambles will grow.'[10] If even brambles will grow on the sites of our future battlefields we shall be lucky.

Particularly important is the advice given in the *Tao Tê Ching* that if arms are used it should only be when there is no alternative, and that one should not speak of their use with relish or exultation. One of the weaknesses of parliamentary democracy is that politicians require votes, and that votes can sometimes be acquired by encouraging people to exult in some temporary technical advantage in the arms race. Little love is ever shown between separate nations, even when their histories are as closely intertwined as those of Britain and France. Yet, as the *Tao Tê Ching* says, the surest defence is 'behind ramparts of compassion'.

The Taoist idea of compassion comes at the highest point on the scale of love, which was described in chapter 4. Compassion is one of the three treasures:

> Now I constantly have three treasures
> Which I hold and cherish.
> The first is known as compassion,
> The second is known as frugality,
> The third is known as not daring to take the lead in
> the empire.[11]

These three treasures need explanation. Not taking the lead is absolutely contrary to the norm in competitive societies. It covers not only taking a humbler seat on a public occasion, as recommended in the New Testament, which we accept in principle, though seldom in practice, but also not pushing in politics, stimulating by example rather than manipulating by force. Even backing into the limelight is unacceptable.

The best of all rulers is but a shadowy presence to his subjects.
  Next comes the ruler they love and praise;
  Next comes one they fear;
  Last comes one they treat with impertinence.
Only when there is not enough faith is there a lack of faith.
  Hesitant, he does not utter words lightly.
  When his task is accomplished and his work done
  The people all say, 'It happened to us naturally.'[12]

'Not daring to take the lead' is the principle behind Taoist statesmanship, strategy, self-defence (in which the onrush of the aggressor is turned to his disadvantage) and personal relations. It is yielding and giving precedence, which smooths relationships, as when two motorists meet on a narrow road, and each urges the other to go first, so that they part in amity and without delay, whereas if each insists that he has priority and the other must reverse, they can be there for hours arguing.

The second treasure, frugality, does not mean cheeseparing. It means not being wasteful. It is a peculiarly Chinese virtue. What the Westerner throws away the Chinese saves and uses. It particularly applies to the wasting of the Earth's resources, the stripping of forests to publish ephemeral or injurious reading matter, or the wasting of food or light or energy for personal display or unnecessary comfort. It includes conservation.

But the first of the three treasures is compassion, or, to use more familiar words from the West, 'the greatest of these is charity', that is to say – Love, but an exalted kind of love. It is a warm word in Chinese, not attractive in sound – *ai* – but warm in its associations of gentleness, loving kindness and sympathy. The Taoists expanded it to include love of the myriad things, of all that is. If one loves all the creatures and plants and exuberance of nature in the way that St Francis of Assisi did, how could one wish to exterminate anything? Conservation is an inevitable development.

The first and greatest of the three treasures can perhaps best be understood by making a comparison. In the West we are taught to think of the good Samaritan as one who loved his neighbour. There he was, virtually a foreigner, finding an unknown person who had been mugged, not in a dark lane, but on the main highway out of the capital. Our own generation would re-gard it as a matter for the police or the social services. 'Don't get involved, man!' But this foreigner fairly stuck his neck out. By stopping he made himself a possible target for attack. By making himself responsible for the victim, he saddled himself with a lot of unnecessary expense. By modern standards his action was heroic; we should place it on the fourth rung of the ladder of love.

There is a story told by Chuang Tzu, however, which may be compared with this one. But it is concerned not only with compassion but with social questions. It was written some three hundred years before the parable of the good Samaritan was told. One of the disciples of Lao Tzu, a courtier named Po Chü, wearing his expensive silken robes was confronted by the body of an executed man .To savour the story one must imagine the courtier in his rich and elegant dress, and on the ground the mangles remains of the prisoner, all blood and guts and terrible stench.

> When Po Chü came to [the State of] Ch'i, he saw the body of a malefactor, drawn and quartered. Binding together the severed limbs, as one wraps a child in its

> swaddling clothes, he took off his Court dress, covered him with it, cried aloud and lamented, saying, 'Oh, Sir, do not think that you will be alone in your fate. Universal is the disaster that has befallen you, though it has touched you sooner than the rest. They say, "Do not murder, do not steal." But it was they who set some on high, dragged others down to ignominy, putting before men's eyes what drives them to discontent. It was they who heaped up goods and possessions, putting before men's eyes what drives them to strife. Set up what drives a man to discontent, heap up what leads him to strife, weary his limbs with toil, not giving him day in day out a moment's rest, and what else can happen but that he should end like this?'[13]

This is very different from the harsh attitude expressed in the Gospel in the words: 'Offences needs must come, but woe unto him by whom the offence cometh.' Yet both Taoism and Christianity in their early days were concerned with the damage done to people by materialistic societies which encourage them to 'heap up goods and possessions'. In particular one senses in Chuang Tzu's narrative Po Chü's feeling of tenderness for the poor mortal remains of the malefactor. The Samaritan faced a different problem where briskness was called for, as the victim was still alive. Yet in the words and actions of Po Chü we can feel something of the Taoist sense of One-ness with all created things, where moral judgments are suspended, and where compassion makes holy that which for others is vile. This compassion makes possible the aspiration towards 'togetherness' which is one of the potent forces helping to shape mankind in the torn societies of the present day. Nevertheless, for all its quietism, Taoism speaks a language of revolution.

It is also worth while to consider the nature of political power. In the West we have given our attention almost completely to the *channels* through which power flows, democratic, oligarchic, plutocratic, authoritarian, and so on. We have paid very little attention to the *quality* of power. But in Taoist thought the situation is reversed. It is the quality of power which is important, for it will find its own channels. In the passage from the *Tao Tê Ching* quoted above, four types of ruler are mentioned, but what differs from one to the other is not really the title or the status of the ruler, but the quality of the power immanent in him. The power that flows from people's personalities is often described in somewhat mystic terms, for how else are we to describe it? But it is no less real for all that. There are some people who command attention the moment they come into a room. Some people approach a bar in a hotel or theatre and are immediately served while others have to wait. It is not a matter of size or physical power. Many of the greatest commanders have been small men, for example Napoleon, Nelson or Montgomery. Some women have such tranquil power that even when old they need only sit on a sofa at a gathering to be surrounded by a circle of friends.

The quality of power immanent in people is different. The *Tao Tê Ching* grades it at four levels. The lowest is that of the person who has so little of it, or it is of such poor quality, that people find it difficult to take him seriously. When such people have greatness forced upon them, they strut and fret. The next level up is the person who inspires fear. At a higher level may be found the person or ruler who does not need to create fear, but who gets things done because he or she inspires devotion. Nevertheless this is still not the highest form of power, for it involves activity. The supreme quality of power is manifested by the ruler who is capable of '*wu wei*' of dynamic non-interference, so vitalising that everyone acts spontaneously according to the rhythms and patterns of the Tao. This is the ideal which follows the stage of benevolent planning.

These four levels of the quality of power are given technical terms as follows: Virtue, Benevolence, Rectitude, Observance of rites. 'The man of superior virtue resorts to no action, nor has he any ulterior motive for action. The man of superior benevolence acts but has no ulterior motive for his action. The man of superior rectitude acts and has an ulterior motive for his action as well. The man superior in the observance of the rites acts, but when no one responds to his action, rolls up his sleeves and resorts to dragging by force.'[14] This phraseology has an old-fashioned atmosphere which seems far removed from the modern world. However, it is extremely relevant, as will soon be made clear. The idea that the best government is one which requires no use of force continued to develop in China, and some fourteen centuries later was expressed by a philosopher writing at about the same time as William the Conqueror was preparing to invade England. His name was Shao Yung. This is what he wrote:

> When we speak of 'empery' we mean non-interference (*wu wei*).
> By 'monarchism' we mean [government by] the use of [reciprocating] kindness and devotion.
> By 'regality' we mean [government by] the use of justice and uprightness.
> By 'usurpation' we mean [government by] the use of sagacity and force.
> Beneath [these we find] barbarism. Beneath barbarism [we find the kingdoms of] the birds and beasts.[15]

The use of sagacity or 'know-how' and force or crude compulsion is the level at which most if not all of the present world's governments operate. They act by observance of such rites as conducting opinion polls and holding parliamentary elections. They may be observed 'rolling up their sleeves and dragging' people, when this is not done by secret ballot but by a rigged show of hands, or by forcing people to vote for three different issues on one voting paper. Such actions lead to the kingdom of the beasts!

What is being set before us in this schematisation is first the idea that the channel by which power is directed is not as important as the quality of power itself, and then that mankind can hope to evolve towards ever higher levels of social living. Today we have some idea of how the societies of birds and beasts function from the many studies made of chimpanzees and other primates, and of other animals lower in the evolutionary scale. Even at the level of the chimpanzees there are rituals of grooming and caressing as a way of overcoming tensions within the society.[16]

Advancing up the scale to the world of men we find that tensions can be reduced not only by hand clasps and gestures, but by talking, and that problems can sometimes be solved not only by force but by discussion. In small societies there then evolves the palaver, the aim of which it to talk conflict out of the problem and arrive at a consensus. This works very well provided that people have plenty of time, and provided that the society is not too big. When the society is too big for everybody to be packed into a hut, hall, or open air theatre, it is necessary to reduce numbers by delegation. In very large and complex societies decision-making was delegated to a supreme ruler and his advisers, or to some other body of manageable size. The problem of the common people was to get or retain some sort of control over those to whom power was entrusted. The ultimate sanction was either to flee in large numbers to some other country, or to rise up in revolt.

The people who migrated into Greece about three thousand years ago seem to have been the first to find a solution to the problem of how the common people were to keep some sort of control over those entrusted with power. This was the ingenious idea of letting everybody who was considered to be properly qualified have a vote and express his opinion through it. When the decision was to be taken, the votes would be counted, and action would then be according to the will of the greater number. This invention cut through endless palavers, and saved an immense amount of time. But it could only be used by societies which had learnt to count, and which could compare numbers. It was a first step towards the mathematisation of politics. During the last twenty centuries this idea has not only spread but has been refined. It worked very well as it was for societies in which all the voters couldbe crammed into a single theatre. When the political unit grew to the size of several million inhabitants, a new development became necessary. This evolved with considerable success in England, where it was found possible for large sections of society to send not delegates but representatives totheir parliament. If a delegate is to put forward the views ofthe people in his constituency it is necessary to have good communications, so that he can refer back when in doubt. In medieval England communications were not good enough for this to be possible. A representative had therefore to be chosen who was believed to be a good man and true, who would do his best in all circumstances, and not have to refer back to those who sent him. Today electronic communication is so radically transforming the scene that it may become possible for an entire population to be consulted, and to vote on even quite small matters, a return in effect to the procedure of the Greek city- states.

Even in countries where the common people do not have much control over their rulers by voting, they are increasing their power invisibly by the spread of opinion polls, and by exerting gentle pressures by writing letters not to the government itself but to newspapers controlled by the government. No government can rule for long in defiance of the wishes of a united population. It is therefore in the interests of governments to find out what people are thinking, and opinion polls and letters to the editor are used no less by the governments of authoritarian countries than by those in more open societies.

Yet all our societies today, open or closed, are still only at the fourth level of power, that in which certain 'rites' may be observed, but the system is really operated by force. There are, however, signs of a move upward to the level of 'rectitude', where not only the rituals of orderly government are carried out, and where justice is administered according to the letter of the law, but where force is less in evidence. The abolition of the death penalty is one indication of this changing attitude. The death penalty is the ultimate in the application of force, but it is often incompatible with the justice that is required at the third level, for if a man is executed, justice cannot be done to him in retrospect if he is later shown to be innocent. Justice at the third level is not fully possible if it is not accompanied by uprightness in all individuals, so that, like Socrates, they would rather volunteer for punishment than see justice injured in any way. Even if a large proportion of the population lived up to these high standards, the state would be poised there in a precarious equilibrium, for the rulers, even though observing a 'superior rectitude' have 'ulterior motives'. For example, if highly motivated to ensure that their party does not lose the next election, the temptation to suppress damaging information, to use their power to hold the election at a time which is disadvantageous to their opponents, or to try to discredit members of the other parties by malicious gossip, may prove irresistible. It is only possible to make a secure advance to a higher level when the population as a whole demands it.

Above the level at which power operates through justice and uprightness there comes the second highest level at which it operates through 'benevolence,' or as Shao Yung interpreted it, through kindness and devotion or loyalty to an ideal. It is possible to see the first sprouts indicating that this form of political benevolence is beginning to germinate even today. This trend may be traced at least to the eighteenth century, with its schools for ragged children. Public works, often selfishly motivated, because the diseases of the poor inconvenienced the rich, spread in the nineteenth century to the people's general advantage, as when cholera was brought under control by the introduction of sanitation. It put out its first blossom with the introduction of the welfare state after the Second World War. It is not impossible that five centuries from now there will be no human beings who starve, are ill with no hope of care, or are totally friendless, anywhere in the world. But it will take time. This type of care must not be confused with doles such as the Romans gave to their dangerous and illiterate mob. There was no benevolence in the act when the Caesars provided bread daily, and circuses every third day, to the descendants of the wretched peasant farmers of Italy, whose farms had been ruined by war, and whose holdings had been bought up by profit-seeking businessmen. The Caesars' motive was fear, and their intention was to keep the mob, which was both huge and violent, as quiet as possible. The Roman attitude is still prevalent today among those who regard the unemployed as wastrels who should be denied their loaf whenever it is safe to do so.

If power is used at the highest level of benevolence it will be because the rulers have no hidden or ulterior motives. This happy state of affairs obviously lies in the remote future. But one should not abandon the ideal that one day government will be completely open. When all individuals can trust each other the very word government will begin to lose its meaning, for the people will not need to be governed if they have other ways of arriving at speedy decisions. This will be possible partly by the use of machines, and partly as a result of altruistic goodwill among all members of the world's population. Although altruism is largely dependent on the economic and moral climate, it is greatly aided in its growth by information. If one has sufficient information to be able to see both or all sides of a question, it is more difficult to press the narrow point of view with conviction. Such a society requires free access to information and the education to enable a person to use it. This was well understood in eleventh century China. Shao Yung's son, in his commentary on his father's work, wrote that at the third level, where government operates through justice and uprightness, the people are admonished by means of equity, but at the next higher level, where it operates through kindness and devotion, they are educated by means of virtue. Information and altruism would seem to be the keys to this desirable state of affairs, where government is becoming quite unobtrusive.

Even this, however, in the Taoist point of view, falls short of the high ideal of non-government, or *wu wei*. The essence of *wu wei*, we repeat, is not to do nothing at all, but to sit quietly and exercise intelligent anticipation. If this is done consistently, problems won't arise. This is expressed in the *Tao Tê Ching* as follows:

> Do that which consists in taking no action; pursue that which is not meddlesome; savour that which has no flavour.
> Make the small big and the few many; do good to him who has done you an injury.
> Lay plans for the accomplishment of the difficult while it is still easy; make something big by starting with it when small.
>
> The difficult in the world must of necessity have its beginning in the easy; the big in the world must of necessity have its beginning in the small. Hence it is because the sage never attempts to be great that he succeeds in becoming great.[17]

There is more to this art of sitting still than meets the eye.

> By not setting foot outside the door
> One knows the whole world.

By not looking out of the window
One knows the way of heaven.
The further one goes
The less one knows.
Hence the sage knows without having to stir,
Identifies without having to see,
Accomplishes without having to do it [i.e.
without having to interfere with the course of nature].[18]

In chapter 16 of the *Tao Tê Ching* it is 'Lao Tzu' himself who is speaking, but it can be taken as a general instruction – Keep to stillness.

I attain the utmost emptiness;
I keep to extreme stillness.
The myriad creatures all rise together
And I watch thereby their return.
The teeming creatures
All return to their separate roots.
Returning to one's roots is known as stillness.
Stillness is what is called 'returning to one's destiny'.
Returning to one's destiny is normal.
Knowledge of the normal is discernment.
Not to know the normal is to be without basis.
To innovate without basis bodes ill.
To know the normal is to be tolerant.
Tolerance leads to impartiality,
Impartiality to kingliness,
Kingliness to heaven,
Heaven to the way,
The way to perpetuity,
And to the end of one's days one will meet
with no danger.[19]

It is easy to dismiss such lines as these as mere mysticism, but in fact they are based on a sharply defined and unflinching view of the universe, not on something fogged-over and misty. It is quite a common experience that the official or officer who complains that people never tell him what is going on is the sort of person who gets agitated. If a subordinate does mention an interesting piece of information, this is likely to be received not in stillness, but with an emotional reaction whose ripples spread far and wide. Coping with such ripples wastes energy. Subordinates play safe and keep their mouths shut. An English monarch who went some way towards understanding the art of stillness was Queen Elizabeth I, watching with extreme vigilance from the centre of her spider's web, restraining when necessary her more impetuous buccaneers, waiting for the moment of decisive action when the Tao was right, and then, with an armament so small that her navy could only find powder and shot for three brief engagements, using tides and winds to secure victory.

That within the apparent vagueness there is a core of clarity is brought out in Chapter 21 of the *Tao Tê Ching*:

> In his every movement a man of great virtue
> Follows the way and the way only.
> As a thing the way is
> Shadowy, indistinct.
> Indistinct and shadowy,
> Yet within it is an image;
> Shadowy and indistinct,
> Yet within it is a substance.
> Dim and dark,
> Yet within it is an essence.
> This essence is quite genuine,
> And within it is something that can be tested.[20]

'Something that can be tested' does not mean subjected to scientific tests, but something that can be trusted and is verifiable. When one begins to know 'the normal' one experiences a flash of illumination, and can then start to understand how it is that things can operate by *wu wei.* Most people experience this a few times in their lives. A tired family with fractious children suddenly find themselves threatened, and 'instinctively' close ranks. The children who only moments before had been exasperating their parents, suddenly become quiet and helpful, and anticipate what is expected of them. The family has become a unit. It was explained in Taoist philosophy by analogy with the human body. The human body, or any other living organism, does not need a king or ruler to tell it what to do. All the different parts of the body work together by some sort of mutual understanding, self-regulating, each part in continuous chemical or nervous communication with all the other parts relevant to it, one part ministering to the needs of another. The Taoist ideal for human societies was to be self-regulating in rather the same way. One occasionally gets this feeling when people are working together for a common purpose and under challenge. It often generates great goodwill. It is also experienced by the members of small military units. Before a battle there is often a period of quiet, the lull before the storm, and during this lull the soldiers carry out their duties spontaneously, without needing to be told what to do, helping each other with a surprising tenderness and quiet concern for one another. I would say this tender concern is one of the best experiences life has to offer.

Yet *wu wei* is in its infancy for the human race. Most people only get occasional flashes of its potentiality during moments of intuition. There would seem to be occasions when group consciousness is operating, but not for long, and often on the dubious fringes of psychic activity, in the areas where established scientists hesitate to risk their reputations. Yet mankind, if it permits itself to survive the next few centuries, can look forward to an immensely long future, during which evolution will continue. Is it likely that in the myriads of centuries which lie before us we shall evolve in body only, and not in brain, and that our brains will not develop improved sensitivities for group communication?

Those human societies which are able to evolve in this direction most rapidly, which are able to order their affairs with the least friction and to communicate with each other most freely and easily, are likely to have an advantage over less gifted societies. It would seem sensible, therefore, to make possible the conditions under which this potentiality can develop, and for a nation to permit the free growth of small groups and societies in which those qualities of mind can be fostered by individuals who have the inclination. The worst thing that could happen would be for the State, with all its power, to interfere with their spontaneous growth by trying in its blundering way to foster them. This would be the opposite of *wu wei* with a vengeance.

Wu wei, to be effective, requires intelligent anticipation. If anticipation is to be effective the judgment must not be clouded by any emotional disturbance. The simile for this in Taoist thought is that the mind should be like a pool of dark water, untroubled by any ripple or wave, which perfectly reflects everything around like a mirror, but also like a mirror, does not retain a reflection once the object has passed. Some swans or geese fly over the pool. The pool reflects them in every detail, but when they have passed, nothing remains. This does not mean that there is no use for memory, but that if, when an event has passed, one retains of it a lingering regret, the sting of remorse, or the residue of old anger, the surface of the pool will be troubled, judgment will be disturbed, and the action taken in anticipation, when problems are still small and easily handled, may be less than intelligent. If the sage allowed his mind to be very distracted, he might not even notice problems sprouting like weeds around him, soon to grow up into robust and poisonous plants.

This dark pool of the mind is mysterious, and we shall return to it in the next chapter. It is preserved by the cult of stillness.

> Can you polish your dark mirror
> And leave no blemish?
> In loving the people and bringing life to the state
> Are you capable of not resorting to knowledge?[21]
> When the gates of heaven open and shut
> Are you capable of keeping to the role of the female?
> When your discernment penetrates the four quarters
> Are you capable of not resorting to knowledge?
> It gives them life and rears them.
> It gives them life without claiming to possess them;
> It is the steward yet exercises no authority over them.
> Such is called dark virtue.[22]

But now inevitably comes the question: 'If the early Taoists had the answer to the world's problems, why have their solutions not been effective?'

There are several answers to this. The first is that no human philosophy is foolproof, and there are always plenty of people wanting to try to wreck the first tentative experiments in innovation. But the second and more important answer is that philosophical Taoism arrived on the political stage rather late. When Taoist ideas first began to grow, China was already in the time of the Warring States, a political jungle. Already the rival states were at each other's throats, and early Taoism, like early Christianity, could only get into the act by changing its nature. Now, after centuries of misguided effort, it is time to think again, not only about Taoism, but about Christianity also. But first perhaps a thumbnail sketch of the rise and decline of Taoism in China will be timely.

China's history, as opposed to its prehistory, begins with its Bronze Age 3,500 years ago. There was then no China, no Chinese people, but two main aggregations, a northern complex and a southern complex of cultures, which included among their diverse interests – from the north, shamanistic religion; from the south or southeast, serpent worship and dragon myths, veneration of sacred mountains, magic connected with the images of dogs made from straw, and spring and autumn mating festivals; from the south, ancestor worship with pig sacrifices. The shamans of the north and the magicians of the southeast contributed much to the development of Taoism, in particular its empathy with the common people, and its willingness to engage in manual work in the preparation of magical substances with the help of cauldrons and furnaces, from which later arose medieval alchemy.[23]

One characteristic of shamanistic religion is the use of trances. Men seem to have discovered at a very early date that useful psychological changes can be induced by dancing, by certain types of music, by suggestion, by rituals culminating in fire-walking, by the breathing of toxic smokes, by narrowing attention to a single point, and by inducing oxygen poisoning or oxygen lack by special methods of breathing. The discovery of alcohol and of hallucinogenic drugs then put into the hands of ordinary people the means of inducing temporary psychological change. Whereas the earlier psychological changes had been induced collectively or under the guidance of 'experts', the discovery of alcohol and other readily obtained drugs made it possible for individuals to treat themselves privately, at home, and without expert supervision. For unstable personalities this could be disastrous.

The inducing of trance states conferred many benefits on primitive communities, in some cases helping them to resolve or reduce tensions within the society, to heal or alleviate certain diseases, to consolidate group feeling, to absolve feelings of guilt, or to come to decisions in time of perplexity. Of particular interest are those techniques, such as that of slow breathing, which enabled people to adopt a different mode of perception from that which they regarded as normal, thereby making available to them the huge resources of that part of the mind which is generally unillumined by the spotlight of conscious attention. To this we shall return. Breathing techniques for this purpose seem to be of great antiquity. Indian yoga and Chinese yogic training have a great deal in common, and are both known to have been practised long before there was direct communication between the two civilisations. Comparable breathing exercises were also practised in ancient Iran, and in Roman Egypt, apparently by transmission from Iran.

Animals survive by learning to identify patterns in the world around them, and on identifying a pattern to take appropriate action. In human beings the faculty of pattern recognition is enormously developed, and everything we experience in our waking hours is selected for attention or is passed through the pattern filter. To get selected and receive attention an experience must first be related to a person's interests, which naturally differ from person to person. For this reason two persons entering a room at the same time will each notice different things. What doesn't interest them is not in fact filtered out completely, but, to be acceptable as part of a pattern, certain other things are required. It is considered normal, for example, that events should occur in sequence along a time dimension; that something which occurs later cannot be the cause of that which occurred earlier, and that events occur as a result of cause and effect. In sleep, however, these conventions no longer apply, and in dreaming we are able to give our attention to things which passed unnoticed through the filter while we were awake. In trance conditions also the usual filtering process is suspended and we experience a different mode of perception.

At an early stage in human history it was discovered that it is sometimes beneficial to suspend the normal process by which we look at problems, and to consider them by a different mode of perception. For example, it was said of the Goths, and before them of the Scyths, that when an important decision had to be taken, such as the declaration of war, they would first debate the issue when drunk, and then again later when sober, and if the decision in each case was the same, the matter was resolved. The early Taoists and other 'mystics' discovered that many of life's problems could be resolved by adopting a different mode of perception. On the one hand this mode of perception narrows down attention to the merest point until the person practising the technique ceases to be aware even of his own body, loses his sense of individuality, and merges with everything else, becoming part of the One. On the other hand, by so doing the field of his general awareness is enlarged so that things are seen in a wider context and therefore in better proportion.

The magicians with their cauldrons and furnaces were one major contributory stream to the general river of Taoism, and the practitioners of withdrawal into a trance state were another. But when society became violently disturbed following the introduction of money and other innovations, the number of people who chose to withdraw from the tensions of society greatly increased. In times of stress there are two types of withdrawal, either solitary or in groups. In religious withdrawal there are hermits living alone, and there are monasteries and convents for those who prefer company. But sometimes withdrawal is the result of political pressure or economic stress. One may then find companies of merry men living in the greenwood, shooting the king's deer and officers, or living the sort of life which Shakespeare idyllically portrays in *As You Like It*, or, as in China during the Warring States period, one may find well-educated people for whom life in corrupt courts had become too dangerous or too unpleasant, withdrawing to the mountains and taking up the hermit life, living of necessity on a spare diet of herbs and dewdrops, and devoting their energies to meditation. From such a background arose 'philosophical Taoism.'

While Chinese society was reacting in this way to the iron hard centuries (600 to 200 BC), a different yet comparable reaction was taking place at the eastern end of the Mediterranean. There the Ionian Greek cities found themselves under stress with the rise of a new mercantile class which challenged the privileges of the old-established families. The whole world appeared to be in a state of flux, and in attempting to deal with it a generation of philosophers arose who, beginning with folk tales and traditional religion, stripped away the magic and the legends, and began to look at the world and particularly at the skies without flinching. There resulted a beginning to science which was to lead to the atom and to that dismantling of the atom which was described in Chapter 2. In China the hermit philosophers also stripped away the magic and looked at the world around them without flinching. But their thinking led them in the opposite direction, not towards the minute components of matter, but towards the inter-relatedness of all that is, towards the idea of action at a distance, and so to the state of mind which can accept the idea of fields of force. Today both types of speculation have come together. Today both atoms and fields are united in scientific thinking.

Neither in China nor in Greece did the era of rational lucidity last very long. In the West the mystery religions came to occupy the centre of the stage, and in China, magicians used the prestige of philosophical Taoism to promote their interests at court. In particular, there was a change in the attitude to death. Whereas Lao Tzu and Chuang Tzu had accepted the idea that an individual comes to an end in body and mind, and is totally recycled, the magicians encouraged the belief not only that life could be prolonged, but that humans could become immortal. If there is no prospect either of an after-life of the spirit, or of being born again in another human or animal body, and if one finds that truly the light is sweet and life worth living, it is natural that people should wish to prolong it. The early researches of the Taoist magicians were, therefore, directed to ways of prolonging life. This is an entirely legitimate aim, one which we ourselves pursue today, and in which, with improvements in medicine and dietetics and in general hygiene, there has been considerable success, with a doubling within a century in some countries of life expectancy. But the Taoist magicians were looking for something more. They hoped to find a drug which would prevent ageing. We hope to find the same thing, but because we now have a certain knowledge of the life processes of cells in human and animal bodies, we have a better chance of finding it.

Several different magical schools contributed to the research. There were those who recommended meditation and the relaxing of the body, those who believed it was important to consume large quantities of life-giving air, those who favoured the type of exercises which came to be known when first introduced to Europe as 'Swedish drill', those who believed in the beneficial powers of sunlight and moonlight, those who believed it was important to achieve harmony of body and mind through a healthy sex life, and recommended sexual exercises, and those who stressed the importance of a healthy diet. In all of this there was a great deal of good sense, but as modern scientific method had not yet been elaborated, a good deal of rubbish was mixed with the sense. The task now is to sift the sense from the rubbish.

Not content with making considerable progress in devising ways of prolonging life, the magicians set their sights higher and aimed at achieving complete immortality. This had great attraction for those who held power, for one way in which power corrupts is by making those who hold it believe that if they give it up it can only lead to disaster for everyone. There were, therefore, great openings at court for those who were able to persuade emperors that they had secrets enabling them to confer on an emperor the gift of immortality. Already one can see a great falling away from the high ideals of philosophical Taoism, in which wealth and influence were the last things a Taoist should seek. But a parting of the ways had occurred even earlier in philosophical thinking.

Assuming that the ideal form of government is one in which the ruler follows the path of non-interference, of *wu wei*, can one be sure that the common people will necessarily respond and do intuitively what is right? Perhaps a short cut to this ideal would be to devise a system of laws so perfect that every eventuality is taken care of. The laws should be absolutely clear, allow of no exceptions, and be enforced with the utmost rigour. The state would then function like a well-oiled machine. This philosophy was known as 'Legalism'.

The philosophical Taoists found they could make no headway at the courts of the feudal princes. Too many people were by this time battling for power and personal advantage. It was as difficult to find a state that was willing in their day to introduce Taoism as a political philosophy, as it was in the early twentieth century to find one which was willing to introduce Marxism. The best hope for a political adventurer was a state that lay on the frontiers of the civilised world. Such a state in the early twentieth century was Russia, and twenty-two centuries earlier such a state lay on the far western borders of the civilised Chinese world. Its name was Ch'in, (*Qin*), the land of the 'terracotta warriors'. This state was soon to give its name to the whole country, and be known to the outside world as China, the Land of the Ch'in.

A number of adventurers made their way to Ch'in in the middle of the third century BC and helped the royal family there to set up a ruthlessly efficient government. Its King became known as Shih Huang Ti, First Emperor, after he had conquered all the feudal states and unified the country into an empire. He ruled it by terror for just twelve years. As he grew older he became desperate for the elixir of immortality, and sent frenzied expeditions to seek it. Shortly after he died his empire collapsed.

The encouragement he had given to Taoist magicians had an effect on philosophical Taoism every bit as damaging as the conversion of Constantine had had on the early Christian church, which then became the enemy of science. Greek science was, however, preserved in some measure by the 'infidels' of Islam, and in time was restored to Western Europe. In China philosophical Taoism was preserved by its devotees hidden away in the forests and mountains.

The success of Taoists in securing the favour of emperors under the Han, the dynasty which followed the Ch'in, led to an increase not in legitimate mysticism, but in deliberate mystification. They appear at this time to have started the belief that the Master of a sect can, after his death, disappear from the tomb, leaving nothing behind but his clothing neatly folded, and then return in the flesh, be seen by his disciples, converse with them, and then disappear again. This was known as *shih chieh*, 'liberation from the corpse'. The first known alleged example of it was performed by Li Shao-Chun, a magician or holy man, approximately 130 years before the birth of Christ. The practice gathered strength. By the year AD 20 the 'immortals' who had practised it were numerous and were subdivided into five different grades. By the mid-fourth century this had been simplified back into three grades. The highest category were able to 'raise themselves up into the aery void'. Those of the second category resorted to famous mountains and forests. The third category sloughed off the body after death and carried on much as before. The process could result 'either in an empty coffin (if the physical frame were fully aetherialised) or in the changeless perpetuation of the adept's body, light in weight like an empty cocoon, and showing no signs of decay after death.'[24]

'Death' among these immortals took the form of disappearing into thin air, the process sometimes being repeated several times; dying but retaining the ability to rap on the coffin; and dying so rapidly that immediately after drinking the elixir of immortality their corpses began to stink. The inverse of this, and hardly more credible, is the story of Lazarus raised from the dead when 'already he stinketh'. The earliest reference to this sort of dying is attributed to Mao Ying of the first century BC. A book, possibly of the seventh century AD, describes how one may know whether 'liberation from the body' has taken place, e.g. by the look of the skin, the light in the eyes, etc., and then goes on to say that there are those who become alive once more after being dead; those whose bodies disappear completely before they are put in the coffin, and those who ascend into the sky leaving only their hair behind. 'Those who effect their liberation during the light of day become immortals of the higher category, while those who do so at night join the company of the lower.'[25]

If one looks at the Western resurrection story through the eyes of Taoist adepts, it would seem that Jesus Christ, whose tomb was already empty by first light except for the folded cloth, must have made his departure during the hours of darkness, and would therefore be graded as a 'lower immortal'. This is supported by the fact that he was seen again in his familiar haunts, which is one of the signs of a 'terrestrial immortal'. Nevertheless, contrary to the Chinese practice, he evidently transferred later to the highest grade, for he was observed to be raised up into the aery void. In the early centuries of our era there seems to have been something of a mania for defying death. To the philosophical Taoists of an earlier and more rational age such stories would have been seen as symptoms of an unhealthy anxiety about one's body and mind, indicating a failure to appreciate man's place in nature.

With the decline of the Han dynasty, some two centuries before the Roman Empire had begun its disintegration, there came the formation of Taoist churches. This seems to have been in response to the challenge of Buddhism from the west, and was marked by the invention of new deities believed to be capable of responding to prayer. The Taoists now developed a Trinity, the Three Pure Ones, of whom the Precious Heavenly Lord controlled time past, the Precious Spiritual Lord controlled time present, and the Precious Divine Lord controlled time to come.

The people in a time of great economic distress turned to the new churches in vast numbers. Contributions were levied from the faithful, in return for healing, making possible the formation of an administrative hierarchy. A large tract of country where the movement was particularly strong, was organised as a political province run on theocratic lines. In due course it challenged the central government, and the terrible rebellion of the Yellow Turbans broke out. Starting in the year 184 AD, about thirty years were needed before it was finally extinguished. This form of Taoism then went underground, and fuelled the countless secret societies, protection gangs and mafias such as persist even today. The Triad Society in London is an example.

Meanwhile, that wing of the movement which consisted of recluses and hermits continued to develop its search for the secret of immortality, the elixir, and the means to transform other metals into gold. From their endless repetitive experiments, and from their records secretively worded but carefully preserved, there flowed a stream of ideas which joined up with the beginnings of alchemy in other lands. Against alchemy and its mystifications there developed only some five hundred years ago the new movement of modern science. The alchemists nevertheless prepared the way for modern chemistry, geology, metallurgy, and – by describing what they observed happening in their crucibles, the marriage of metals, and so on, in Freudian terms – contributed ideas for modern psychiatry; those of the recluses, on the other hand, who were more interested in immortality than gold, prepared a wealth of information concerning vegetable and mineral substances which were absorbed into the developing sciences of botany and mineralogy with their practical applications in pharmacy and medicine.

Among scholars the great books of philosophical Taoism continued to command respect, even when the rest of Taoism had become riddled with superstition and charlatanry. Thinking men were still absorbed with the great question of how an individual should see himself in relation to the rest of the universe, and how best he should identify with the One. Age after age men followed the advice given in the *Tao Tê Ching* to 'return to the root'. The aim of the next chapter will be to sift some of the ideas which have been thrown up by Taoism over the centuries, and see which are still valid today and may be used to help us find a way out of the wilderness, back to the root.

REFERENCE NOTES

Chapter 5.

1. For a description of people still living in the 'golden age', the three hundred remaining Nemadi of Mauretania 'who hunt and smile,' see Chatwin, (1987) pp.143–48.
2. The story is found in Chapter 4 of *Lieh Tzu*, and is here quoted from Needham (1952), Vol.2, p.142, but adopting some phrases from the translation of Graham, (1960), p.102.
3. Quoted from Idries Shah (1969) p.136.
4. *Tao Tê Ching*, Ch.67. D.C.Lau (1982), p.243–5.
5. *Tao Tê Ching*, Ch.69. D.C.Lau, p.247.
6. *Tao Tê Ching*, Ch.31. D.C.Lau, p.315.
7. *Tao Tê Ching*, Ch.68. D.C.Lau, p.245.
8. *Tao Tê Ching*, Ch.30. D.C.Lau, p.313.

9. *Tao Tê Ching*, Ch.31. D.C.Lau, p.315.
10. *Tao Tê Ching*, Ch.30. D.C.Lau, p.313.
11. *Tao Tê Ching*, Ch.67. D.C.Lau , p.243.
12. *Tao Tê Ching*, Ch.17. D.C.Lau , p.291.
13. Waley (1939), p. 105.
14. *Tao Tê Ching*, Ch.38. D.C.Lau (1982), p.189. c.f. also the version he gives on p.57.
15. Shao Yung, *Kuan Wu Wai P'ien*, (B), fol. 19b. Trans. author.
16. Richard Dawkins has spoken (BBC 15th and 19th April, 1986), on the rewards of grooming and the mechanics of competition between 'cheats', 'grudgers' and 'suckers'.
17. *Tao Tê Ching*, Ch.63. D.C.Lau (1982) p.231.
18. *Tao Tê Ching*, Ch.67. D.C.Lau p.203.
19. *Tao Tê Ching*, Ch.16. D.C.Lau p.289–91.
20. *Tao Tê Ching*, Ch.21. D.C.Lau p.31–33.
21. 'Knowledge' here is a technical term meaning knowledge of the procedures of feudalism concerning status, precedence, etc. See Needham (1954) Vol.2., p.86 ff.
22. *Tao Tê Ching*, Ch.10. D.C.Lau (1982) p.279.
23. See Needham (1954), Vol.1, pp. 89-90.
24. See Needham (1954), Vol.5, pt 2, pp. 106, 284 and 296–7.
25. Related in fourth century AD Ko Hung's *Pao P'u Tzu*, ch.2, trans. Needham (1954), Vol.5, pt 2, pp. 296–8.

6

The Way Re-opened

Taoism contains a pearl hidden by the incrustation of centuries. Taoism was once a philosophy and a contemplative way of life. Then it was transformed into a religion, with militant churches fostering mass emotion and magic-mongering. Then it began to take part in violent politics, as did the Church of Rome in the Middle Ages. Once this happened the Way was lost. But in many a scholar's study or in quiet retreats in the mountains the old Way continued to be followed, for the three great books remained – first the *Lao Tzu,* writings from various sources, periods and authors, attributed to a mysterious Master Lao, but evidently given lyrical shape by someone with an intimate understanding of the ruthless politics of the closing years of the period of the 'Warring States' of China. This was originally two works, the Classic of Power and the Classic of the Way, later made into one book, the Classic of the Way and of Power, the *Tao Tê Ching.* Then the *Chuang Tzu,* the writings attributed to the humorous, teasing, lyrical Chuang Chou. Then we have a third work, the *Lieh Tzu,* compiled some time during the fourth century AD from earlier sources, but presenting the main ideas of the old Taoism in a new form following the dreadful upheavals and slaughters which were the birth pangs of China as a united empire. This is perhaps the best of the three books with which first to become acquainted with Taoism, for, as A.C. Graham says in the introduction to his translation: 'The Western reader of this book, struck first of all by its naïve delight in the irrational and marvellous, may well feel that no way of thought could be more alien to the climate of twentieth century science. Looking more closely, he may be surprised to discover that Taoism coincides with the scientific world view at just those points where the latter most disturbs Westerners rooted in the Christian tradition – the littleness of man in a vast universe; the inhuman Tao which all things follow, without purpose and indifferent to human needs; the transience of life, the impossibility of knowing what comes after death . . . 'You are the breath of heaven and earth which goes to and fro, how can you ever possess it?'

In each of these three books there is an insistence on returning to the 'root'. Let us begin with a famous passage from the *Lao Tzu*, which is as rationalist for its age as any modern scientist could hope to find:

> (In the beginning) there was something
> undifferentiated and yet complete
> Before Heaven and Earth were produced,
> Silent! Empty!
> Sufficient unto itself! Unchanging!
> Revolving incessantly, never exhausted.
> It is capable of being [has the potential to
> become] the mother of heaven and earth.
> As yet I do not know its name.
> I style it 'the way'.
> I give it the makeshift name of 'great'.
> Being great it is described as receding,
> Receding, it is described as far away,
> Being far away, it is described as turning back.

> The ways of men are conditioned to those of earth,
> the ways of earth by those of heaven,
> the ways of heaven by those of the Tao,
> and the Tao came into being by itself.[1]

The Taoist thinkers were concerned with the great problem of holism, that once the whole is splintered and you begin to analyse a fragment, the fragment ceases to be what it was, just as a slice from the body of an insect when seen under a microscope is no longer what it was when it formed part of the living insect. As soon as a thing is isolated and observed the situation is altered, for the observer is part of the experiment. This was expressed in the opening words of the *Tao Tê Ching* as follows:

> The way can be spoken of,
> But it will not be the constant way;
> The name can be named,
> But it will not be the constant name.
> The nameless was the beginning of the myriad creatures;
> The named was the mother of the myriad creatures.[2]

To understand this we need to think of the origin of the universe as we now believe it to have happened. Our starting point, as described in Chapter 2, is taken as an immense concentration of energy in which the interactions were undifferentiated. The concentration was unstable and resulted in 'The Big Bang', in which that which had been highly concentrated began to expand, and in expanding lost heat. As it cooled the One lost its symmetry, and the four interactions – gravity, and the strong, weak and electromagnetic interactions, became differentiated.

We can give a name to part of this process – The Big Bang – but because it can be named, it does not name anything constant or eternal, but on the contrary something that changes all the time. From this developing explosion have come all the phenomena of the universe, interactions, elements, molecules and organisms, combining, recombining and proliferating in endless permutations until no further energy can be released. In the poetic language of the *Tao Tê Ching*, The Big Bang would be 'the mother of the myriad creatures'. Of course in those days they were not able to visualise atoms consisting of protons and the particles which perform their unceasing dance around them. But they were able to visualise some cosmic event from which everything else could have developed, and both Ionian and Taoist philosophers at about the same time arrived at world views which were to lead on to modern science.

But where did this Fireball, this unstable concentration of energy, come from? The language of physics at this point becomes difficult for the layman to follow, and full of paradoxes. Before the Fireball was the void, but a void full of potential. What part did randomness play in the building up of that concentration of energy which resulted in the Fireball? From this pregnant Nothing came the One. The Nothing and the One can both be spoken of, but once one of them can be named it is no longer constant. As the last lines of the same chapter of the *Tao Tê Ching* express it:

> These two have the same origin but differ in name.
> They are both called dark,
> Darkness upon darkness
> The gateway to all that is subtle.

We must be content to leave it at this, for once it is possible to apply a name to what we observe it has ceased to be potential.

When the Taoists speak of this endless processing and reprocessing as 'the Way', they are not giving it a real name, but are referring to it as 'the way in which . . .' In English we might refer to the Tao as 'the How'. The How in Taoist thinking meant that there is, beyond the reach of ordinary language, the great Void, the Nothing, but, as in modern physics, it is a void full of potential. They believed that the basic material of the universe was continuously being created or appearing from the void, and continuously disappearing back into it in an endless cycle. This material they called, *ch'i*, (or *qi*). On first appearing it would be extremely tenuous and 'subtle', but it could become more and more solid and hard until in agglomerations we would recognise it as rock or heavy metals. In time it would become tenuous again, and would finally disappear back into the Void. *Ch'i* was therefore thought to exist in two modes, expanding and contracting. Heaven and Earth had been formed from agglomerations of *ch'i*, the hardest and heaviest forming the core of the Earth, the lightest composing the air and vapours that blow above it. Where the two modes were most perfectly blended, organic life appeared, and naturally man was believed to be a particularly harmonious blending of the two. These two modes of being were described as Yin and Yang, originally two quite primitive terms used to describe the shady side of a hill and the sunny side of a hill, as explained in Chapter 1, but gradually enlarged to include all sorts of opposites such as hot and cold, hard and soft, male and female, and developed into a proto-scientific system.

'Tao gave birth to the One; the One gave birth successively to two things, three things, up to ten thousand [i.e. everything].'[3] When the One became differentiated, it produced two modes, and *ch'i* when produced in one or other of these modes, Yin or Yang, was capable of combining and recombining in countless permutations, and so of producing by expansion and dispersion, (the Yang mode), or by contraction and agglomeration, (the Yin mode), everything that is known to us in the universe, and everything still unknown, which the Chinese referred to as the 'myriad things'. This, in brief, was the world view of the Taoist philosophers. Like that of the Ionian philosophers, it cannot claim to be modern science, but it can claim to be a rational attempt to explain things without recourse to the supernatural.

Although their science must be updated, the attitudes generated by a rationalist attitude to the universe are completely modern. First of all, man is not singled out for any special favour by a creator God, but is just one of the myriad things that are the result of evolution. Nor is there any suggestion that man has been given dominion over the world of nature. The whole emphasis of Taoism is on symbiosis and mutual respect, which, in the enlightened members of the human species develops into love for all that is. Respect for the world of nature and for the How of things generates the attitude which we now call 'conservationist.' But conservation is directed *against* the ravages of the selfish and the witless. When things follow their natural Tao and men are illumined by intelligence the matter of being against ravages does not arise.

Another very modern attitude in Taoism is the equality of the sexes. Yin and Yang balance each other. There is no question of the dominance and exaggerations of the one being replaced by the dominance and exaggerations of the other, with violent swings of the pendulum, although a mild oscillation is inevitable. But what is desirable is balance, for it is when Yang and Yin are in balance that together they are most fruitful. The fecundity of the Tao is expressed in its endless permutations. It is not a matter of profit or advantage. If it were so the Tao would only produce those species that are likely to turn out to be good investments of energy. But the Tao produces its myriads of creatures in restless abundance, regardless of whether they will succeed or fail, be efficient or inefficient, useful or useless, beautiful or ugly. It is quite untrue that everything in nature was created with an end in view, let alone in order to be useful to man. The Tao has proliferated birds, for example, of unguessable varieties – the superb peacock whose fan of feathers draws the attention of the hunter to the target, the Argus pheasant with its splendid tail handicapping it as it races away through the jungle, and the poor booby doomed to extinction. According to the Tao everything is worth trying once. It loves and welcomes within the cosmic laboratory every type of freak, sport and eccentric, every new shape of leaf and combination of colour. It grows the poisonous deathcap toadstool as a passable likeness of the edible mushroom. It proliferates bacteria and viruses, both benign and malignant from the human point of view. The Tao has no point of view. The sick, the crippled, the deformed, the insane, all have their place in the Tao, all are of interest. For those who delight in the Tao even to be disadvantaged is perfectly acceptable. This is how Chuang Tzu expressed it:

> Soon Master Yü fell ill, and Master Ssu went to enquire.
>
> 'Wonderful! how the maker of things is turning me into this crumpled thing. He hunches me and sticks out my back, the five pipes to the spine run up above my head, my chin hides down in my navel, my shoulders are higher than my crown, the knobbly bone in my neck points up at the sky. The energies of Yin and Yang are all awry!'
>
> His heart was at ease and he had nothing to do. He tottered out to look at his reflection in the well.
>
> 'Ugh! The maker of things still goes on turning me into this crumpled thing.'
>
> 'Do you hate it?'
>
> 'No, why should I hate it? . . . This is what of old was called 'being loosed from the bonds'; and whoever cannot loose himself other things bind still tighter. And it is no new thing after all that creatures do not prevail against Heaven. What would be the point in hating it?'[4]

This attitude to sickness and deformity foreshadows the Taoist attitude to death. It is not an attitude of fatalistic resignation to the inevitable, nor of fear or of morbid curiosity, and certainly not a belief that like a little child one will be gathered up in the arms of a fond parent, or directed to a happier land, or sent to judgment to be followed by reward or punishment. It is a little like the attitude of Socrates, finding equally satisfactory the possibility either of total obliteration or of the continuation of personality and the possibility of meeting others and enjoying the pleasure of discourse. Arthur Waley has written of the Taoists' 'lyrical acceptance of death'. This lyrical acceptance of death is possible because of their lyrical acceptance of love during life. Hui Tzu wrote, 'Let your love spread to all the myriad things, heaven and earth are one unit.'[5] There was much discussion in ancient China as to whether universal love is possible. Before such a question can be answered one must be clear which level of love is being talked about. In Chapter 4 love was analysed at five different levels. Love of the myriad things begins to come into its own at level 4, and identification with the One is achieved at level 5. Mo Ti's belief in universal love for one's fellow men was based on love at level 4. The Confucians, who felt that one could not possibly love everybody in the way in which one loves the members of one's family, were thinking of love as something nearer to level 3. The love of the Taoists for the myriad things was near to the compassion of the Buddhists for all the creatures everywhere whom they believed to be the victims in a world of illusion.

Yet though Taoism and Buddhism had much in common, and in the case of Zen Buddhism actually fused together, they were poles apart in their attitude to life, the Buddhists regarding the world as utterly insubstantial and illusory, and something to escape from – the enshrinement of the death wish, whereas the Taoists regarded the physical universe as the real thing which had evolved from nothing, and which would return to nothing, perhaps evolving again, Buddhist-like, in endless cycles. But reality is the here and now, to be accepted as a rare gift, and enjoyed while it lasts, the ultimate in optimism. When one's time is up, one's 'destiny' fulfilled, one doesn't argue or throw tantrums with the benign host who made it possible, but hands over all temporary possessions, making room for others. But if this brief experience is to be enjoyed to the full, one must cultivate an inward stillness so that one's perceptions are not blunted or perverted by any distraction.

In cultivating this inward stillness, we extend the area of perceptivity, communicate more freely with the myriad things, and increase our joy in the experience. There is not much time in an average life to do this. Assume a person lives for 70 years. It takes him the first 25 years to get properly oriented. From his 26th birthday he can look forward to some 45 years of activity. This means an expectation of 540 months. But a third of this time will be spent asleep, and another third may be spent at work of such a nature that he has no opportunity to cultivate inward stillness and extend perceptivity. This means that from the age of 26 onwards he may have only the equivalent of 180 months or even less for his most important activity. Our time is short.

> One moment in Annihilation's waste,
> One moment from the well of life to taste.
> The stars are setting, and the caravan
> Starts for the dawn of Nothing. Oh, make haste.

But it is only possible to speak of 'Annihilation's waste' if one gives undue emphasis to the importance of an individual.[6] The universe into which he is absorbed is seething with creativity. To regard the passing of an individual as annihilation is like regretting the fleeting impermanence of a wave on the surface of the enduring ocean. Nor does the caravan start for the dawn of

Nothing, for cities lie beyond the desert. Yet the mathematician Omar Khayyam, to whom FitzGerald's verses are attributed, was right to stress how short is the time for any individual. If he is to discover the pearl that will illuminate his life, he cannot afford to lose any time at all. Yet there is no greater distraction from its discovery than the emotional disturbance caused by anger or jealousy or the excitements that are generated by competitive ambition, let alone the madness that goes with cruelty or racist hatred.

Cultivating inward stillness and communicating with the myriad things are both aspects of the One. 'In the most ancient times men and animals lived together and walked side by side. In the time of the Five Emperors and the Three Kings, the animals were frightened away and scattered for the first time. In our own degenerate times, they crouch in hiding and flee to their lairs to avoid harm.'[7] These words from the *Lieh Tzu* written nearly 2,000 years ago, no longer tell the whole story. Today animals can no longer even flee to their lairs to avoid harm, for the countryside where they had their lairs is ripped up and turned into plantations or eroded into desert or drained and dug and covered with concrete. As Confucius would have said, 'Alas, how great is our decay!' We read of those who are said to have been able to summon animals into their presence as if this were something in the realm of legend – Orpheus in ancient Greece, Music Master K'uei in ancient China, King Solomon with his ring, and even St Francis of Assisi. Yet even today such things are performed by those who have kept something of the art of stillness. It is still possible in Borneo, in the swamps where protein is scarce, to set out in search of food with a crocodile hunter in his frail canoe, by night through overgrown muddy creeks, with an oil lamp for a light and a silk thread for a lassoe. The crocodiles' eyes glow in the light of the lamp, the hunter intones his pre-Islamic incantations; very quietly the crocodile of his choice drifts alongside the canoe, and very quietly the hunter places the silken thread around its jaw and back over its head. Gently he tightens the noose and very gently the crocodile drifts behind the canoe as the hunter paddles back home with his catch.

Lieh Tzu speaks of an art of fishing which is not so dissimilar, and which uses stillness and concentration of mind to achieve success, as do the Stone-Age hunters of Australia who can enter the waters of a lake so quietly as not to disturb a flock of ducks, and swimming beneath them drag down by their feet as many as they need for food.

> Chan Ho made a fishing line from a single thread of silk out of the cocoon, a hook from a beard of wheat, a rod from one of the pygmy bamboos of Ch'u, and baited it with a split grain of rice. He hooked a fish big enough to fill a cart, in the middle of a swift current in waters seven hundred feet deep. The line did not snap, the hook did not straighten out, the rod did not bend, because he let out and drew in the line following the pull and give of the water.
>
> When asked by the King of Ch'u to explain how he did it, he replied,
>
> 'When I overlook the river holding my rod, there are no distracting thoughts in my mind. I contemplate nothing but the fish. When I cast my line and sink the hook, my hand does not pull too hard nor give too easily, so that nothing can disturb it. When the fish see the bait on my hook, it is like sinking dust or gathered foam, and they swallow it without suspecting. This is how I am able to use weak things to control strong ones, light things to bring in heavy ones. If Your Majesty is really able to rule his state in the same way, he can turn the Empire within the palm of his hand; what can give you trouble?'[8]

This is, of course, a political parable, but it draws perhaps on a tradition of Stone-Age fishing skills.

These skills still exist, but they are vanishing fast. It may still be possible to witness the calling of the porpoise on Pacific islands, the calling of the shark to the shores of the Indian Ocean, and it is not yet three generations since the government in Lagos forbade the people in what is now Cameroon to call the whale, because the agreed price for so much meat was one young man who every year entered the water to offer welcome along with the rest of the people, but did not return.

Men did not always 'walk with animals side by side' in order to take some of them quietly or by compact for their food. Often it was to prevent damage, and for this the men of the elephant society in Cameroon would 'become elephants' and go out to greet a herd that was dangerously near their village, and persuade them to go elsewhere. But the spiritual exercises, the fasting and the dieting that precede such transformations are incompatible with the daily routines of office life, and – though our camera skills are teaching us much more than was known before *about* animals – our empathy *with* them will soon be as remote as the tales of were-wolves or the pied piper of Hamelin. Perhaps in India for some time yet cobras, deaf yet not insensitive to music, will be persuaded by the sound of fluting to come from their holes and dance, enabling the snake charmer, with a flash of his hand to seize them behind the hood, and no doubt people who are interested in such things will always, if they have patience and a little stillness in their hearts, be able to lie out among the rocks on a hot day, and persuade lizards to join them simply by whistling. Perhaps before it is too late our Stone-Age empathy with animals may be recovered, but this is unlikely for as long as they are sent in droves to our slaughter-houses, to be butchered without dignity or respect. To take an animal's life for much needed protein does not in itself offend the Tao. We are all part of the food chain endlessly recycled. But to take an animal's life unnecessarily and for greed, and to despatch it as part of a machine process, ignominiously and without respect, is an affront to the Tao for which there will certainly be a response. It is unlikely that large animals will ever again be able to threaten us, but the Tao is not mocked. Infinitely small creatures are evolving more quickly than we can pursue them. Such new diseases as AIDS are perhaps indicators of how the pendulum will swing.

Skills may be lost, but there are many aspects of mental powers still living within us which, though severely atrophied, may yet be revived. Our sense of smell, for example, though never as keen as with some animals, operates far below its true potential due to neglect. Yet sometimes women when pregnant recover their ancestral sense of smell in an astonishing way, and know when an odorous substance is being used in the house even though they may be several rooms away from it. I once experienced a recovery of my sense of smell in an unforgettable manner. I was walking along the Roman road from Bath to Wood-stock, experimenting to see how little equipment I could manage with when sleeping out. In this case it was a sheet of plastic, a ball of string, some newspaper, food, water and matches. On the high ground above Bath I could see a storm approaching from the Bristol Channel, so I prepared my place for the night among tall oak trees which were growing in an old quarry. It was a wild night, and the huge trees swayed and thrashed above me like bushes. Being alone I was once more in a primeval world in which survival depends on the acute functioning of one's senses. When I woke up after a night of unconscious alert I was unaware of any change in myself, but when my walk was over and I was back at home, I was amazed to find that all the familiar things about me had a smell, even such things as glasses and plates which I had long regarded as normally odourless. Yet after just one night in a bed under a roof I found that this newly recovered faculty had vanished.

Another faculty which becomes atrophied from our dependence on machines is our sense of time. If we are without a watch or clock, we look for substitutes such as the position of the sun, or signs from the regular rhythms of daily life. But we have within us biological clocks which are more reliable than night porters at some hotels, as air travellers sometimes discover. Then there are some races of men who seem to have preserved a sense of direction within them, almost as if they had a built-in compass to aid them in their direction finding, as have some birds and fish. There is a whole area of the mind which seems to respond in unusual ways that present problems for mechanistic logic. These areas cover pictorial visualisations and the fringe subjects which reputable scientists steer clear of, such as water 'divining' and telepathy. All these it is convenient to consider as activities of the Yin mind. It is now, therefore, time to reconsider the Chinese concept of the Yin and the Yang, and to make clear how much of it, if any, is scientifically acceptable.

Whenever a situation occurs in which something is disturbed from an intermediate position, but forces tending to restore the changing matter to its intermediate position are exactly proportional to its displacement from that position, then a curve of harmonic variation is generated. For example, the concentration of sunlight falling on the Earth's northern (or southern) hemisphere will follow a rhythmic fluctuation which may be expressed as a curve of harmonic variation. The intermediate position may be visualised as a time line. A curving line may be drawn above and below this time line, in the form of a continuing wave, like the letter S drawn on its side – in other words a sinusoidal curve. The points where this sinusoidal curve are at their maximum distance from the intermediate line indicate the two solstices, when there is a maximum concentration of sunlight on a given area in summer, and a maximum dispersal of sunlight in winter. The two points at which concentration and dispersal are equally balanced are when the curve cuts the intermediate or time line, indicating the equinoxes of spring and autumn.

Coordinate geometry and the use of graphs have only grown up during the last five hundred years. At the beginning of our era the Chinese did not have the mathematics to express such ideas by means of sinusoidal curves. What they said was: 'When the Tao of the Yang has reached its summit, then the Tao of the Yin takes over the task; when the Tao of the Yin has reached its summit, that of the Yang in turn takes over.'[9] At the time of the winter solstice, at the very instant when the Yin was at its maximum, the Yang began to take over, and day by day grew in strength. At the time of the summer solstice the opposite occurred. The Yang began to wane and the Yin to increase in strength. When the terms Yang and Yin are used to describe this sort of behaviour of observed phenomena, there is nothing unscientific about it. But it is no longer very useful, for coordinates and the ability to express with the help of graphs things developing along a time line offer us a far better method of description.

The term 'Yin and Yang' or 'Yin-Yang' was also used to mean 'forces'. The Yin was thought of as a force that moulded matter, the universal stuff, in such a way that it would become compressed, cold and inert, whereas the Yang had the opposite effect, causing matter to be rarified and hot, like burning gas spurting from a lump of coal. There were, then, according to this theory, in fact four forces, the Yang waxing and the Yang waning, and simultaneously the Yin waning and the Yin waxing. It was rather as if Laplace, in attempting to account for the phenomena of the universe in terms of gravity, had had to take into account positive gravity and positive anti-gravity, and also negative gravity and negative anti-gravity. Although Laplace explained the universe to his satisfaction with recourse to only one gravitational force, the twentieth century made it clear that there are four forces to be reckoned with, that of gravity and the three interactions, strong, weak and electromagnetic. Early Chinese gropings in the direction of the idea of forces are, however, utterly different from modern conceptions of force, and need no longer occupy our attention.

The term Yin-Yang, then, when used to describe certain forms of cyclical behaviour, is acceptable but superseded by improved methods of description, whereas when used to mean positive and negative forces it is scientifically unacceptable. A term does not, however, have to be used scientifically in order to be useful. The word 'wind', for example, is very useful, but quite unscientific, in the sense that it cannot be precisely defined, as Karl Popper has shown.[10]

At what speed does a body of moving air become a wind? If one decides, for the purpose of definition, that air moving at 10 kms per hour is a wind, is air moving at 9.999 kms per hour not a wind? And for how long does it have to sustain this motion for it not to be classified as a gust? And how much air is needed for it to constitute a 'body' when one is talking of wind? Yet in spite of this it would be difficult to write a weather report without the word 'wind'. It is a very useful word. Similarly the term Yin-Yang is very useful for describing the sort of dualism which, unlike the ancient Iranian or Zoroastrian dualism, does not carry with it a moral judgment on the two classes of things which are summarised by the dualist classification. As it has become urgent to break the habit of classifying opposites with a built-in moral judgment, the term Yin-Yang is very useful, because once the term is understood one knows that the classes referred to are both regarded as neutral, and if it is a matter of cycles and recycling, it carries no implications of doom, hell and judgment.

One area where fear and moral judgments persist is in classifications concerning the mind. We speak quite freely today of the conscious and the unconscious mind, together with a peculiar shadowy borderland known as the subconscious. Logic is held to be an operation of the conscious mind. That which is logical is good. That which is illogical is bad. This belief would seem to be more highly prized in France than in England. In England many people have a vague idea that if a project is too logical it's bound to get snarled up. One gets into even deeper water with art. A painting may be quite illogical, and yet be a very good painting. Everyone responds to the art of Bosch, yet what he paints often defies the logic of the waking world.

The logic of Bosch's paintings is often that of what we may unscientifically call the Yin mind. An example would go like this: The body is a house for the soul. A house may be made of shell. A snail, for example, lives in a shell house. If shell is used as a material for houses, the soul could be housed in an eggshell. A man's body may therefore be portrayed as an eggshell. If an eggshell is broken, we can see what is inside. As the eggshell body is a house, we shall be able to see people inside it. If the soul is evil, the people living in the eggshell house will be evil. The eggshell house may therefore be portrayed as a tavern full of debauched people. The fact that the man with the eggshell body and the revellers in the tavern are drawn to different scales is irrelevant. Who said that everything must be artificially constrained within a single frame of reference?

The answer to that question is 'the Yang mind.' From the moment that we become conscious, which may be a month or two before birth, we are exposed to an unceasing stream of sense impressions. As soon as a baby's sense of hearing is sufficiently developed, it is exposed to a tremendous uproar of noises inside its mother's body, the ceaseless banging of her heart, the soughing of her breath, the gurglings of her digestion and the occasional whoosh of her plumbing, not to mention the orchestra playing upstairs when she speaks or sings. In addition there are many sounds which come in from outside. All this receives attention, but it is the subject matter for only one single sense – hearing. The other senses are also developing. The act of being born precipitates a child into a bedlam of new impressions. From the most tender age it must begin to select those few things out of an enormous total to which it can reasonably pay attention.

Furthermore, every animal's survival depends in large measure on its being able to pay attention to those things which are most important to it. If a thing is to receive attention it must be recognised. If it is to be recognised it must form a pattern. The Yang mind is concerned with focusing attention like a spotlight on the ever shifting blur of impressions provided by the senses, and matching them against records of earlier impressions stored in the memory, to see if they make a recognisable pattern. If they do, a swift decision is needed to grade them in importance and give each pattern a priority for possible action.[11] If a pattern is judged to be unimportant, the spotlight is switched elsewhere. That does not mean, however, that the pattern is totally disregarded. The Yin mind may also be interested. But if the Yang mind is to do an efficient job in pattern recognition and decision making, it must not be distracted by constant shifts in the frames of reference with which the decisions are made. The Yin mind is not placed under the same constraints. When the Yang mind pays attention to the details of Bosch's eggshell man, it would say to itself something like this: 'These things don't exist. A man with an eggshell body does not match up with my previous experience of the world. The whole thing is impossible because . . . (logic, logic.)' In order to appreciate the picture we have to call in the Yin mind as a consultant. With some people the Yin mind is scarcely used except in dreaming. In their waking hours they are completely dominated by the Yang mind. They would dismiss Bosch's picture as rubbish. They are said to have little imagination.

Imagination or 'picture-forming' is an important faculty of the Yin mind. The Yang mind cannot create pictures. It can create diagrams, sketch maps and perhaps very simple outline pictures, usually monochromatic, but it cannot create a picture in abundant detail and vivid colour such as we see in dreams. Oversimplified books on Yoga will tell you that it is possible to create pictures in the mind by concentration. This is impossible if the Yang mind is used. A picture established by looking at an object will fade within three seconds of closing the eyes if it is left to the Yang mind. To see pictures in the mind one must learn to release the Yin mind from the domination of the Yang. Artistic people, daydreamers and mystics have the knack of doing this. The ideal to aim at is a good balance between the Yang mind and the Yin.

Another example of the working of the Yin mind is to be found in the memory. Normally we memorise things with the help of the Yang mind. We make mnemonic connections like stepping stones across a river. For instance, a kind and jolly man was once introduced to me whose name was Chandler. He had three double-chins forming rolls of fat, like tallow. Candles are made from tallow. Chandlers make candles. His name was Chandler. Six months later I met him again, and had no difficulty in recalling his name. It instantly came running across the stepping stones in my mind. But sometimes we fail to make mnemonic connections, or they break down. After struggling to remember a name or fact we give up, and say, 'Never mind, it'll come back.' What we are doing is handing over the retrieval process to the Yin mind, deliberately relaxing and allowing it to do its work, while the Yang mind gets on with its next job. Then, quite without warning, some ten minutes later, or in the middle of the night, or even after quite a long interval, the Yin mind suddenly comes up with the answer. It may be a telephone number, or an address we haven't used for twenty years, or a detail from childhood long 'forgotten'. The important fact is that to enlist the help of the Yin mind, it is necessary to relax.

If one thinks in terms of dualistic forces eternally at war, the Yin mind will be thought of as an enemy. Certainly in the remote past of the peoples of Western Asia and Europe, that which was not under conscious control was thought of as a dangerous region, dark and shadowy, the haunt of witches, demons and monsters, the region of madness to which one only descends if accompanied by a supernatural guide, or firmly grasping some magical plant or talisman. But if one accepts the Yin-Yang view of life there is no conflict but a healthy alternation and a quest for balance. The Yin mind is our friend no less than the Yang. But our civilisations for the last four thousand years have been hopelessly out of balance, grossly exaggerated in favour of the Yang, the male, the strong, the hard, the conquering. It is time to redress the balance and cultivate the Yin.

In a Yang-dominated life the only time when the Yin mind can give us the benefit of its advice is in times of dreaming, when the Yang mind has switched off its spotlight and is no longer engaged in pattern-seeking activities. Messages from the Yin mind must, however, be interpreted according to Yin rules. If one attempts to interpret a Yin message according to Yang rules it will seem to be mere rubbish. Because the rules are different, what seems in a dream to be hilariously funny turns out on waking to be rather stupid, and vice versa.[12] The Yin mind is not interested in linear time. People long dead can operate as if time did not exist. It is not interested in mechanistic cause and effect. Things can happen spontaneously. It is not interested in keeping things in rigid compartments. 'Logical' barriers are readily broken down. If one remembers that the Yang mind's way of interpreting events is extremely specialised and artificial, and does not apply to the messages of the Yin mind, the messages of the Yin mind can be interpreted.

It should not be thought that the messages of the Yin mind are always going to be dramatic and important. Many of them are rather boring reminders that one is under stress and would the Yang mind please do something to reduce it. This may not be possible, but there's no harm in being reminded. The greater the stress the more insistent the dreams become. The Yin mind sometimes puts up suggestions as to how stress could be reduced or problems solved. On waking, the Yang mind dismisses them as rubbish and carries on as before. But it would be sensible to recognise them as distress calls, and see if something practical cannot be done. For example, I was once under stress when my wife was in hospital, since, in addition to my day's work I was also visiting her there, and looking after the house and animals. My Yin mind drew attention to this stress by composing a dream in which, during my visit to the hospital, the ward sister very kindly said she had arranged for me to have a bed next to my wife, and that it would be perfectly all right for me to keep the dog under it! Although the Yin mind expresses its anxieties in ways which the Yang mind knows are impractical or ridiculous, it would nevertheless be possible to recognise from such reminders the cause of the anxiety, and perhaps to arrange for a neighbour to feed the dog and reduce the stress. The Yin mind is our friend and is there to help us.

We have spoken of the Yin mind as having a back-up memory retrieval system, as having powers of visualisation, and as providing early warning of stress. In addition it operates the kind of skills which cannot be taught, but which come to us by some sort of intuition, and which are destroyed by the interference of the Yang mind. Taoist writings are full of references to these skills and knacks.

There is, for example, the story of Tsao-fu learning the art of charioteering from his father. First his father set up a row of posts, just big enough to stand on, and the length of a stride apart. Tsao-fu had to practise running backwards and forwards, striding from one post to the next without stumbling. After three days he could do it perfectly by what we would now call conditioned reflexes. The Yang mind was no longer required to give his running any attention. As Lieh-Tzu expressed it: 'You responded with your mind to what you felt in your feet.' But this was only the beginning.

His father then went on to describe the minute sensitivity which develops between hand and mind, or between mind and any other part of the body, such as gave rise to the story of the archer Kan Ying who could receive an arrow in flight between his teeth.

> Applying this to charioteering, you must control the bridle from the point where it meets the bit, and pull tight or slacken, feeling the corners of the lips; decision must come from within your breast and execution from within the palm of your hand. What you sense within in your innermost heart will accord outside with the horse's temper. In this way you will be able to advance and withdraw treading a stretched cord, and wheel round as exactly as a compass.

To appreciate what follows it is necessary to imagine an ancient Chinese chariot. They were extremely light, with dished wheels having many spokes. Normally they were pulled by two rather small horses, but sometimes by four, and occasionally even six horses all running together, side by side. To control six horses in pairs running in file is difficult enough. When they are in line abreast it is much more so. Roman chariot races were usually run with one pair of horses pulling a chariot, but sometimes two more horses were used, not bridled but attached only by a trace on the outside. With the Chinese six-horse chariot all were bridled. This meant that the charioteer had to hold in his hand at least twelve reins, and in making a tight circle each horse would have to feel a different degree of pressure on the mouth if the charioteer were to make a perfect circle as from a compass. Tsao-fu's father then continued as follows:

> If you respond with the bridle to what you feel in the bit, with the hand to what you feel in the bridle, with the mind to what you feel in the hand, then you will see without eyes and urge without a goad; relaxed in mind and straight in posture, holding six bridles without confusing them, you will place the twenty-four hooves exactly where you want them, and swing round, advance and withdraw with perfect precision. Only then will you be able to drive carving a rut no wider than the chariot's wheel, on a cliff which drops at the edge of the horse's hoof, never noticing that mountains and valleys are steep and plains and marshland are flat, seeing them as all the same.[13]

There are many activities which share with charioteering this dualism of the mind, the Yang and Yin. In giving lectures and making speeches, for example, one may begin by enlisting the aid of the Yin mind in suddenly seeing connections between facts, or in juxtaposing them in such a way as seems amusing or causes surprise, or in conjuring up felicitous phrases and quotations, but after that the Yang mind gets to work in knocking the whole thing into logical order, reshaping and abbreviating for clearly understood reasons, and in memorising points of connection or transition. Winston Churchill's great speeches were apparently made this way, a preliminary inspired period, followed by several hours slogging work. It is difficult to believe that he ever said to himself, 'What I need here is a good quotation suggesting that people are going to have a bad time and they'll have to put up with it. Let me just look through the dictionary of quotations. Ah! These lines from John Donne seem to be what I need!' Surely his Yin mind, not focused on one small problem, but brooding largely over the tremendous issues at stake, ranging backwards and forwards through history as if time were all one present, and swooping every now and again on things he had heard or seen or read, suddenly fell on the words 'I have nothing to offer but blood, toil, tears and sweat,' and knew that they were right. But sometimes a lecturer will exert his Yang mind first, collecting his raw material for his talk, but not put it into final shape until he sees his audience, for his audience may be an unknown terrain, and like a skilled charioteer he must drive this way and that, with as sensitive a rapport between him and them as there was between the Chinese charioteer and the cliff's edge by the side of which he must place the twenty-four flying hooves of his horses.

It is not in the arts only that we draw on the wealth of the Yin mind for inspiration. In science also many of the greatest discoveries have transcended logic. When Kepler first began to feel a conviction that there was 'a force in the sun' which moves the planets, he was sustained not by logic but by the picture-making powers of the Yin mind through analogy. He saw the sun as it were manipulating a broom by its handle and sweeping the planets along. The logic and the calculations came later. But the inspiration came like a flash from a lighthouse in the shadowy Yin regions where the spotlight of the Yang mind never penetrates. Einstein's ideas for the formulation of the special theory of relativity also came to him as sudden realisations transcending logic, and Chu Tsai-Yü in China, a contemporary of Shakespeare, after wrestling a long time with the problem of how to express the tuning of the equal-tempered scale mathematically, relates how he woke one morning at dawn and in a flash realised what had to be done.

Why should it be necessary to labour the point, which can be well-expressed in more familiar terms, that the human mind works through inspiration as well as logic? Why is it necessary to write at length about the Yang and the Yin? The reason is that Western civilisation is a fragmenting civilisation, divisive, disruptive and polemical. Our thinking is guided towards fragmentation by the nature of the languages we use. David Bohm has warned of the dangers facing such a civilisation, and has stressed the need for holism if civilisation is to survive.[14] One can begin the mending process with language, and the Yin-Yang concept is a powerful aid towards holistic thinking. The point about the civilisation of classical China is that it was a holistic civilisation, and many of the terms used in traditional Chinese thinking, even when they point to contrasts, stress complimentarity rather than opposition. In the West logic is the opposite of intuition. But the Yang and the Yin in the operations of the mind complement each other, and the most successful operations are those in which they work in partnership and achieve a balance.

A future book will explore a way by which individuals may find a holistic view of life and achieve a balance. We are not concerned with reviving an antique form of Taoism long past its prime, but with abstracting from it ideas which are still useful, and combining them within a framework of modern science in such a way that we obtain a new view of the world we live in, which will carry us forward for a time until yet another formulation is needed. As Mao Tse-Tung said, 'We must make the past serve the present.'

Let us now review what Philosophical Taoism has to offer, and then consider how people of the twenty-first century can turn these ideas to account. The majority of the world's population will, before long, be living in enormous cities. How can these ideas be put into practice?

When Taoism was first formulated two thousand five hundred years ago, human populations were sparse, and it was not difficult for a person who wished to cultivate the spiritual side of his nature to retire to some lonely spot in the mountains or by the seashore, and there meditate or carry out alchemical experiments in solitude. Today it is difficult to escape from the noise of traffic, jetplanes, telephones and mechanical music. Obviously new arrangements are needed.

First let us re-emphasise that Taoism was not originally a religion but a way of life with a great sensitivity to the numinous in nature. It recognised that when the One-ness of things is fragmented, when the 'uncarved block' is split, and countless small things are considered in isolation, meaning becomes distorted, and degeneration sets in. This degeneration was already far advanced before Taoism was formulated as a philosophy, though of course an ideal state of One-ness had never really existed, but was projected into the neolithic past, with its primitive technology, instead of into the future, where advanced communications technology may make it possible.

Nevertheless this early philosophical Taoism did stress the importance of living a non-materialist life, avoiding ambition, rivalry and all types of competitiveness, not wishing to become famous, withdrawing early at the moment of success, and leaving others to claim the credit, not demanding status or prizing the outward signs of it, setting no store by wealth or luxury, loving the people in a curiously dispassionate way, serving them but not asking for any reward, stressing that the meek shall ultimately inherit the earth, for power has within it the seeds of its own destruction, just as the Yang contains within it the seed of the Yin. Much of this is familiar from the New Testament – new, that is to say, some five centuries after these ideas had been current in China.

Now these ideas may be considered in a new setting. One-ness is taking an important place not only in physics[15] but in society. The poetic conception of the Yin-Yang ebb and flow of life may now be better suited for the future of mankind than the eternal warring of factions promoted by ancient Iranian dualism. Total lifelong commitment to a single cause does not necessarily command respect now, as the label 'a good party man' once used to. It suggests inflexibility and perhaps prejudice. Now is the age of the floating voter.

Our attitude is already changing towards work. Many in the West are appalled at the Japanese industrial ethic by which a young man or woman enters a factory or business and is expected to stay in it all his or her life. In the West the tendency is the opposite – to make it easier for people to move around by enabling them to transfer their pension contributions from one job to another. If this trend develops we may find people holding contrasting jobs at different times of the year. The idea is already spreading: a ski instructor in the winter and a beach guard in the summer; a restaurateur in the summer and a supply teacher in the winter. Ideally the Yin-Yang rhythm would indicate a period of intellectual work to be followed by a period of physical work, an extrovert period of hassle with people, such as is experienced by those who work at complaints counters, airport check-in desks, lost property offices and welfare offices, followed by an introvert or at least quiet period working with plants or animals, at calculation or in research. Perhaps ideally the year should be divided into a period when one does highly specialised, exacting and well-paid work involving decision making and responsibility, and the use of one's intellectual abilities, contrasting with a period when one works for a low wage or for nothing on a welfare job requiring dedication to the common good. Between these would come a period when one's work is creative rather than administrative, a period for growing things or making things or for creative and artistic activity. But no less important is it to have a period of spiritual retreat and refreshment, and a time for shaking off 'the dust of the world' and seeking identification with the One.

The most remarkable attempt to get such a rhythm going was made in China in the last years of Mao Tse-Tung, when intellectuals were sent to the countryside to work with their hands for a period, and to learn to identify with the peasants as a step towards building the *Ta-t'ung*, the 'Great Togetherness', which was the ancient Taoist term for a classless society. It was not a great success for reasons now obvious. In the first place it was carried out on an enormous scale in quite a short period of time. To succeed such an experiment requires great dedication. There were certainly many instances when a university professor learnt from the peasants and they from him, but many others when he was lost in an alien countryside, and they despised this man who could not carry out the simplest agricultural tasks properly. In such an experiment everything depends on a sympathetic and sensitive relationship. This is unlikely to be achieved as a result of large-scale government planning, particularly if it is used as a punitive measure to break the spirit of dangerous intellectuals. If a government wishes to establish the Ta-t'ung, the Great Togetherness, by introducing a Yin-Yang social rhythm, the best thing they can do is by example to alter the climate of opinion, and then to *wu-wei*, to avoid interfering but let the people make their own arrangements. It may be that by legislation they can remove obstructions to this process, repealing antiquated laws and so on, but the very least they can do is to avoid being obstructive in new ways.

If for our spiritual well-being it is necessary from time to time to withdraw from the hurly-burly of the Yang world, how is this to be done? The traditional method, first developed by the Buddhists, was to withdraw to a religious house for a period of silence and meditation. This is still in use, and in Buddhist countries it would not be considered eccentric for an active politician to go into retreat for a time, and to emerge better able to deal with his problems. Some groups of dedicated people have tried to establish an unaggressive way of life in communes in isolated places. These are sometimes established in clear opposition to the Tao of the locality. For example, the islands that fringe the coasts of Britain have become more and more depopulated during the twentieth century, and many of them are now inhabited only by rabbits or puffins. The reason why people have abandoned them is because the economic tide is absolutely turned against them if they wish to bring up families and remain in the present. There are a few people who wish to spend their whole lives on lonely islands, but they must be prepared to accept the economic standards of the early Irish monks, living if not on puffins, then on potatoes.

But this sort of dedication is not realistic. It is typical of the extreme form of dualist thinking to imagine that one's entire life must be spent under such conditions. It is not a question of all or nothing. There is after all such a thing as a shift system. Groups of like-minded people can arrange to retire in turn for perhaps three months in the year from the stench and noise and tension of great cities, and live and work on their lonely island for a shift, co-ordinating their individual and group activities, and then, when their Yin period is nearing exhaustion, return with new zest to the Yang life and the wider community.

There does seem to be a rhythm in human history, with some periods when records are compiled, and others when they are analysed. Very often a long period is necessary before the records are sufficiently complete to make analysis possible. In the former period information is digested. In the latter proofs are formulated. There are periods when the Yin mind sets the tone, with its emphasis on intuition, inspiration and One-ness. These are followed by periods of individualism, separation and analysis, when the Yang mind sets a premium on personal strength. The Yang phase in Europe would seem to be drawing to a close, proliferation of highly individual nation states, each aggressively pursuing its interests, being no longer so useful. Women now have more influence in affairs, as they did in the Roman Empire when the peak of male aggressivity had passed; and there are signs of two types of diplomacy at work, the tough Yang diplomacy of governments, and the gentler Yin diplomacy of the Churches. History, however, is a sort of poetry, constructed in the minds of those who look backwards in time, and

Yang and Yin rhythms are also poetic constructions. Such poetry must not be mistaken for science, and used as a basis for predicting likely outcomes. Even science itself is a sort of poetry, being constructed from a relatively small selection of observations extracted from a huge total of related phenomena. But we like the poems we are used to, and find it a shock to observe what we regard as natural laws being defied. This occurs, for instance, when we see the sun rising in the west, while we are flying to San Francisco from London via the near Arctic night. The same sort of shock was experienced by Carthaginian sailors when they observed the sun to their north, and by modern rationalists when confronted by phenomena described with little justification as '*super*natural'.

Poetry, however, whether in the form of scientific interpretation, mathematical constructions or verbalised imaginings, helps us to draw closer to the One, though our understanding of the One can never be more than an approximation. When an approximation breaks down there is a period of stress before it is replaced by a new one. For example, there was a One-ness in the days of Christendom which made people feel secure. When it began to break down there followed a period of stress, one symptom of which was an outbreak of witch-hunting and witch-burning through all Western Europe. The feeling of loss and bafflement was also expressed by John Donne in the seventeenth century, in his poem 'Anatomie of the World', "First Anniversary", part of which reads as follows:

> And new Philosophy calls all in doubt,
> The Element of Fire is quite put out;
> The Sun is lost, and th'earth, and no man's wit
> Can well direct him where to looke for it . . .
> 'Tis all in peeces, all cohaerance gone:
> All just supply, and all Relation . . .

Today our sense of bafflement and frustration is even greater, as the loss of 'cohaerance' seems to be pulling the world to pieces. It is not surprising that people turn to the old Bronze-Age religions for comfort, or ask what the stars foretell, or throw themselves into the acquisition of goods, or allow their concentration to be drained away by the mindless permutations of commercial sport. A new view of One-ness is overdue.

Yet another component towards a new view of One-ness will, however, be provided by education. There is a Yang type of education with which all in the West are familiar because it is compulsory. In the West it owes much to the ideas which made the Roman army victorious. The Latin word *disciplina* originally meant learning in the broadest sense, and was later narrowed to mean training, and then took on the overtones of military training with its emphasis on authority, obedience and savage punishments. Beating children is characteristic of Yang education all over the world. It was a not uncommon feature of Confucian education in traditional China. It was a feature of the education of boys in West Africa when they met for instruction in hunting and tribal customs under their chief. It was accepted as normal in Europe until recent times. At the age of eight I was told that if I had not mastered the cases of certain Latin nouns by the next day I would have my bottom beaten till it was 'as red as raw beef, and as raw as red beef'.

The essence of Yang education is that it is highly planned, highly organised and often compulsory. It stresses logical processes, step by step progression, and thrives on repetition. It sieves people, puts them into categories, and, by excessive stress on examinations, risks amputating part of the mind. It proved itself excellent in its day for producing conscientious civil servants and governors of colonies. The list of brilliant people who suffered under it, struggled through it or did without it is endless. Shakespeare and Winston Churchill are examples of people who struggled through it without distinction. Charles Darwin was 'found to be slow' at school. He went to Shrewsbury School, and recalled it as 'simply a blank'. Albert Einstein was another 'slow child'. He disliked the regimentation of regular schooling. There are of course some temperaments which thrive under the Yang type of education, who need the security of defined frontiers and a disciplined timetable. Marie Sklodowska, the wife of Pierre Curie, performed brilliantly during her perfectly orthodox high school education. Her husband on the other hand is a perfect example of one who benefited from a Yin type education. He never went to school, but studied at home, taught first by his mother, then by his father, and later privately studying with a professor of mathematics. By these unorthodox routes it was then possible to enter universities. They are now almost completely blocked, putting the Yin personality at a disadvantage.

The essence of a Yin education is that it is voluntary, the learner being led on by interest and his own motivation. It is informal, what is learnt often being absorbed unconsciously. It is unregimented, continuing all through life for as long as the learner's mind is open to new ideas. It seems that all that is needed to get a Yin learner going is an understanding of the principle by which words can be represented by letters, and numbers by figures. With their feet on the first rung of the ladder, really intelligent children can then climb on their own. For example, William Cobbett, the great nineteenth century radical thinker, was taught to read by an elder boy he knew, and all the rest of his education was acquired from the books he read, and the people he spoke to. Niccolò Tartaglia, who took part in public debate with Italy's leading mathematicians of the sixteenth century, and made so many contributions to mathematics, ballistics, and a wide array of subjects, came from a family so poor that his widowed mother could only afford to pay a teacher to teach him the letters of the alphabet as far as the letter K. With that his formal education ended, but it was enough. He learnt the rest for himself, was later appointed professor of mathematics in Venice, yet, characteristically for that hard age, died alone and in poverty.

The Chinese philosopher Mencius is another example of a boy who had no schooling, but was taught to read by his mother. Benjamin Franklin's formal education consisted of less than a year in a grammar school, before he was put to soap boiling at the age of ten, but two years later he was indentured to a printer which gave him a chance to read. John Dalton, born in 1766, illustrates a fluid mix of Yin and Yang in his education, for he went to a village school, but an enlightened Quaker school, where he climbed the first few rungs of the ladder, leaving at the age of twelve to start labouring. Fortunately at the age of fifteen he secured a job as an assistant teacher in the school at Kendal in Cumbria. It had a small but useful library, some stimulating scientific equipment, and a flow of visitors by stagecoach on the road from Scotland to London, who were persuaded to give lectures to the school. With the help of his friend John Gough he made himself proficient in Latin, Greek, French, mathematics, botany, astronomy, chemistry, medicine and other subjects to the level of his time. The Yin learner is nothing if not an all-rounder. From this base he proceeded to elaborate the atomic theory in chemistry.

The key moment in Yin education is when the pupil finds his *guru*. Because their temperaments are matched there is a free flow of ideas. When this happens even in formal schooling the results are good. When they are not matched it can be disastrous. What is needed is to devise a way by which it can happen more often. We cannot recapture the fluidity of the wandering scholars, but it may be possible to establish a new type of social unit, which might be called the 'flexible family', where a Yin education would be as natural as that which occurs in ordinary families where children learn informally from their parents. The flexible family would be a group of people, not necessarily related, but who have the loving concern for each other that the best families have. Such groups would assemble a diversity of talents and qualities, and would meet from time to time to study the Tao of living, to produce articles which cannot be economically produced in factories, to carry out research in areas which powerful organisations neglect, to 'love the people' invisibly in the Taoist manner, and to perform small ceremonies promoting One-ness. For such people life would become a journey through a marvellous countryside. Not everyone would wish to leave the security of the city he knows, to make such a journey. Those who do would think of themselves as travellers rich in experience, travelling light. Of this there will be more to say in the last chapter.

REFERENCE NOTES

Chapter 6.

1. *Tao Tê Ching*, ch. 25, tr. Needham, (1954). Vol.2, p.50, and Lau D.C., p.303.
2. *Tao Tê Ching*, ch.1, tr. Lau, p.267.
3. Waley, (1934), p.195.
4. Graham, (1981), p.88.
5. This is to be found in the last chapter of *Chuang Tzu* called 'Below in the Empire.' Hui Tzu's paradoxes are listed, but this, the tenth, is not a paradox, but a Taoist affirmation. See Graham (1981), p.9 and pp.283–4.
6. Western writers have long been obsessed with the fear of the individual getting lost in the wasteland. Compare, for example Andrew Marvell: 'And yonder all before us lie/ Deserts of vast eternity.'
7. Graham, (1960), p.55.
8. *Ibid*, pp. 105–6.
9. Needham, (1954), Vol.4, Pt 1, pp.6 ff.

10. Popper, (1945) Vol.2, pp. 17–18.
11. The mechanism by which a human individual makes a decision is still imperfectly explored. Some help may be had from Vickers' *Decision Processes in Visual Perception*, but Singleton, (1989), p.208 says: 'The human process of making a choice between alternatives in the context of incomplete information . . . remains obscure.' He realises that there is great pressure for clarification of the human process by designers of information technology, but in spite of this 'progress remains slow'.
12. Here is an example of a 'hilarious' dream which I recorded: Returning in my car from a party I was approached by a policeman armed with a breathalyser. He said, 'Are you driving home?' To which I wittily replied, 'No, I'm a hiving drone.' On waking the dream rapidly lost its humour due to its inherent improbability, defective spoonerism, and disruptive use of the indefinite article.
13. Graham, (1960), p.114.
14. See David B. Bohm, *Wholeness and the Implicate Order.*
15. *Ibid*, p.134.

7

A Mechanism for Immunity

People who live in the technically advanced societies are under continual pressure from machines. This point was made at the very beginning of this book, and now we may develop it a little further. In his book *The Great Amphibium* (1931) Joseph Needham described how the continual appearance of arbitrary facts expressed in quantitative form, and absolutely devoid of living interest can be seen everywhere around us. 'It is as if the human mind were fascinated by the coils of accurate nonsense which it is for ever spinning.' Meaningless statistics dominate our thinking. 'What is needed,' he wrote, 'is a mechanism that will immunise us against the peculiar mental bias associated with a life surrounded by machinery.' But what form would such a mechanism take?

Until a few centuries ago people who lived in towns would have been surrounded by tools and contrivances of various sorts, but not by machinery. To see a relatively complex machine in action you had to observe a clock or visit a windmill or a watermill. There were of course plenty of horses and carts, but life was not dominated by them as it is today by machines. If a mechanism was needed to counter the pressures of living, religion provided it. That mechanism was the sacred year pursuing its course from feast day to feast day – Christmas, Easter, Lammas, Hallowe'en – apparently undeterred by the discoveries of astronomers and inventors. Yet not to be so indefinitely.

The battle with machines had in fact already been lost centuries before, when citizens started listening for the chimes of the tall town clock rather than for the church or monastery bell rung for matins or angelus, which, till the fourteenth century had been the undisputed timekeeper. Then, little by little, but ever more swiftly, clock time began to regulate the lives of men, and factory time to enslave them.

As Needham said back in 1931: 'The old prestige of Church, Aristocracy, Classical Learning, etc., etc., has gone and can never return.' The Church itself, being based on untestable premises, on faith, can do little to immunise us against the peculiar mental bias associated with a life surrounded by machinery, with its ruthless logic of mechanical cause and effect. Indeed, the Church itself is now a prey to statistics and high technology. If we wish to immunise ourselves against the mental bias associated with a life surrounded by machinery, it is no good looking back to the old Bronze-Age religions. We must look forward to something quite different.

It is here, as so often in so many ways, that China can provide us with new ideas from right outside our own tradition. To take an example of how this has happened in the past, China some 3,500 years ago organised its numbers on a decimal place system, five myriad four thousand three hundred twenty and one being written as 54321, which was far simpler than the Roman system of LIVMCCCXXI. Naturally this system eventually swept the board, and when the people of Cambodia, not later than the eighth century, added a circle to indicate that a place was empty, the system of Chinese-Indian-Arabic decimal place numbers complete with zero was ready to become the international number system such as we use today.[1]

To take another example, every country in the world has borrowed the Chinese system of promoting the most suitable person for a job by selection after examination. Before the Chinese examination system was introduced into the West in the nineteenth century, the usual way to get a job in government service was through the good offices of an uncle or friend in high places. Now we use impartial examinations not merely for selecting civil servants but for grading people wherever grading is necessary. It is from China that we have borrowed this idea of grading.

The Chinese also took to machines quite early. The Romans had an abundant supply of slaves, and for them the simplest way to increase production was to increase the number of slaves on the job. The Romans showed little mechanical inventiveness. But by the sixth century the Chinese had found a better way than using slave power. They had mechanised spinning and weaving, pumping, stamping, crushing and working bellows with the help of water power, and had combined many different operations in one factory from a single power source. Though their machine age began so early, they did not have Luddite uprisings, or grossly despoil the countryside; not until, in recent centuries, overpopulation and pressure on the land began its lethal work. One reason for this was that their attitude towards nature and the acquisition of wealth held machines in check. They had a mechanism.

This mechanism was perhaps in the end a little too efficient. Properly controlled labour saving machinery can be benign, helping the weak and feeding the hungry. Out of control it becomes a scourge. The Chinese court and bureaucracy so feared this scourge that they strenuously resisted 'modernisation', especially the building of railways, and held back the tide for some fifty years. Had Taoist philosophy been dominant, rather than Confucian, they would have allowed the tide to run its course, channelling it to those areas where its effect would have been benign. The result of un-Taoist action was to destroy the stability of the state, and to smash the ancient mechanism which had safeguarded China for so many centuries.

This mechanism was essentially a calendar designed to keep man in close touch with nature, and responsive to its changes, showing every aspect of nature as interlinked in one gigantic unity. It evolved gradually during the centuries before our era, and was recorded in the form of a book entitled *Yueh Ling* or *Ordinances of the Months.*

The Chinese thought of the universe as something that ebbs and flows, waxes and wanes, expands and contracts for ever. The power inherent in the universe may be seen in the unending cosmic dance. To take advantage of this power and perhaps channel some of it for human benefit, it was necessary for men everywhere to study the ebb and flow, the *Yin* and *Yang* of things, to follow the Tao, and sometimes then, perhaps, to channel a little of it for their use.

At the very apex of the pyramid of human endeavour stood the emperor, the pontifex, the bridge builder, the mediator between heaven and earth. This was symbolised in the ceremonies which were held at the Temple of Heaven, when the emperor ascended to the highest level, above all the court officials and the common people, to prove by his example that they were worthy to receive the celestial power which would reinvigorate the earth so that it would 'bring forth abundant crops and many sons and grandsons'. Today we use not gods or emperors but atomic reactors to mediate between heaven and earth, hoping thereby to confer blessings on mankind.

Science has grown with alarming speed. Religions everywhere have been obliged to rethink their premisses, and either adapt to the new scientific environment as best they can, or atrophy. In Imperial China the adaptation was left too late. The emperor was driven out, the magic was destroyed and the ancient mechanism collapsed.

Let us consider the pressures on us today. First there are clocks everywhere reminding us second by second of 'the unforgiving minute'. Time is our invisible master. Then, resulting from the invention of the clock, there are the timetables, schedules, diaries, calendars, programmes, plans of work, progress reports, returns, tax demands and so on, which make up the framework within which we are obliged to live, allot our attention, and divide our leisure. Then there is the physical impact of machines – the overwhelming, almost inescapable noise they produce, the roar of traffic, the scream of planes during take-off and landing, the blaring of unwanted music, the shattering sounds of high-powered machines doing their necessary work of construction, destruction or repair. Then there is the toll of machines on human bodies – those killed or injured in accidents, those whose health is affected by rays, vapours and toxic substances. Though machines are wonderful servants for man, in complex situations they dominate us. The flexible family suggested in the last chapter should contrive to arrange such a pattern of living for its members as will give them respite from the pressure of machines not by taking equally high pressure holidays, but by following the *yin-yang* rhythm of activities throughout the year. This is the mechanism which we must develop if we are to acquire immunity against machines and the pseudo-science which they foster.

Most groups of thinking people are well aware that our present civilisation, the result of some six thousand years of sacrifice and effort, is extremely fragile and may easily be swept away by catastrophic events resulting from war, disease, climatic change, overpopulation, exhaustion of resources, the complexities of urban life, or economic collapse. We may visualise small groups of survivors in isolated pockets, their machine- made clothes falling to pieces, their machine-made shoes coming apart, without matches, tools or protection against the weather. For their survival certain prehistoric skills and inventions would be essential – fire making, for example. But who now in the industrial societies can make fire without help from modern technology? It is not simply a matter of rubbing sticks together and fire appears. To get fire by friction is exceedingly difficult. Lucky the man after a collapse of civilisation who has developed the skills and learnt how to acquire the blessing of fire in good time. Among such men would be many thousands of devout Hindus who still make fire as a sacred ritual by ancient methods.

It would be a wise precaution, therefore, if thinking people form groups to plan ahead, to decide what are the essentials of our civilisation which need to be preserved at all costs, even through a period of barbarism after the collapse of civilisation, and to enshrine them in rituals which would preserve them, like seeds for some future harvest, through the dark winter of world catastrophe. Stories and traditions soon become distorted and inaccurate, but precise rituals carefully observed are capable of transmitting ideas into the far future. They should therefore be part of the discipline of the group, helping it to survive.

One aim should be to help bring man closer to nature. That closeness was readily felt in the Middle Ages but was shattered as scientific understanding of the natural world became more and more complex, and as man's mastery of nature became more and more securely established. In the days when a man's health was believed to depend on the balance of his humours, and when the world was believed to be compounded of only four elements – earth, air, fire and water – problems could be explained in such simple terms that even for uneducated people there was an evident coherence. Today it is impossible to return to such simple scientific explanations, but it may be possible to introduce a new coherence by grouping the world's complexities not according to 'elements' but under the five great blessings of air, water, food, fire and earth. Air is the first great blessing. Deprived of it for only a few minutes we die. Water is the second blessing. Without it we can live for only a few days.

Food is the third. Without it we can live for only a few weeks. Fire is the fourth. Without it we could not survive in cold climates, nor have achieved a technological civilisation. Earth is the last great blessing. From it comes all our food and wealth. To it we all return. Under these five blessings can be grouped all the world's complexities according to poetic and aesthetic analogies. The use of such analogies was highly developed in traditional China. They are set out in the *Yeuh Ling*. Its analogies and correlations linking, for example, fire with the sun, the south, the colour red, the summer season, feverish illnesses and so on, were much derided by Europeans, since these were not scientific correlations.

Our greatest loss since the Middle Ages is perhaps, in the words of John Donne quoted in the last chapter, 'cohaerance' in our view of the world and the universe. Before the Renaissance everything had its place and men knew where they stood, or thought they did. Their world then collapsed. It was followed by a world of machines over which we have only partial control. Eventually with increasing knowledge and great effort a new cohering world image will emerge. But this will only result from strenuous effort to rethink our philosophy, religion, law, politics, ethics, and our social structures and arrangements. The task which confronts us is at least as great as that which confronted the men of the Renaissance when they were faced by what Immanuel Wallerstein has called 'the four collapses'[2], the collapse of the feudal order, of the State, of the Church, and of the Mongol Empire with its great trade routes running from the China Sea to the Mediterranean ports, right across Central Asia.

Such rebuilding may well take centuries. First, all the world's great civilisations need to be seen in relation to one another, and in relation to what they have contributed, and can yet contribute to a one-world civilisation. Even collecting information for this has barely begun. A real understanding of the civilisation process has only just started. It is only within the last few hundred years that we have even become aware that our world is part of just one of millions of galaxies; that man has evolved from simpler life-forms; that the illnesses he is prone to are not inflicted on him as punishments for sin; that his 'mind' is a complex fiction used to help us describe workings of the brain which we don't yet properly understand; and that looting and murdering foreigners is not necessarily the best way to sort out complex economic and social problems. We are right at the beginning of the process of civilisation, just emerging from what the ancient Taoists called 'the kingdom of the birds and beasts', that is – from natural savagery. There are bound to be setbacks. But at least we now have a vision of one holistic world.

Next we may look at our modern societies. In many ways they are less successful than the primitive societies of earlier times. A society cannot be regarded as successful if it carries on its back a high proportion of hungry people, of old people who lead lonely lives under great difficulties, of young people who find themselves trapped in an existence without home, work or hope, and of people who are sick or in pain who cannot get medical help. In many parts of the world this is accepted as the natural way of life.

Hitherto the family has been the most rugged and enduring social structure. Most parents will fight desperately, and will deny themselves endlessly, to protect their young. But one family is too small a unit to be viable on its own. We therefore find family units combining in a wide variety of complex organisations – clan, tribe, nation and so on, which give family units a better chance. A successful version of this is the 'extended family' in which those with a common ancestor help each other with food, money, shelter or political influence whenever called upon. To refuse to answer an appeal for help in such societies is unthinkable. But it means that the most gifted or successful or energetic members of the extended family are called upon most often for help, and find it most difficult to rise above the average level. It is they who pay the price. The extended family has a built-in brake on its progress. The obligations of the extended family being onerous, its members try whenever possible to disappear into another type of social organisation which is less demanding. One such organisation is the 'nuclear family', which has grown up in the Western world following the Industrial Revolution.

The Industrial Revolution offered people, especially women, a previously undreamed of variety of jobs, enabling the nuclear family – parents and children – to survive on its own within the more complex organisation of the nation state. The nuclear family has obligations to the nation state, but only in very reduced degree to anyone else. When the extended family exists in a rapidly modernising nation state, individuals, especially in towns, lose no time in weakening their obligations to the extended family and setting up as nuclear families. The extreme form of the nuclear family is the single parent family.

There are, however, drawbacks to the nuclear family. The burden of looking after old people which was formerly shared by a large number of relations all living in one house, or close by, now falls perhaps on two children or sometimes on just one unfortunate daughter who is trapped in that heavy and often thankless task until death brings release. The atmosphere in a nuclear family is also often highly charged with emotion, because when there is a quarrel it cannot be dissipated among a large number of participants with many different points of view, but must be fought to a conclusion between the main antagonists – husband and wife. Under these circumstances it is not surprising that divorce should be frequent and that children unable to endure the tension should leave home.

The nation state has tried to remedy this by building up the welfare state so that the obligations which are no longer carried by the extended family and are too much for the nuclear family can be undertaken by the welfare department of the bureaucracy. A family, however, has an intimate understanding of the idiosyncrasies of its members, which a bureaucracy can never have. An extended family can call its rebellious or scrounger members to book. The two parents of a nuclear family, unsupported in dealing with a difficult child, usually cannot do this; still less can the clerks in a bureaucracy. What would seem to be needed is a new type of family structure, which in the last chapter I called the 'flexible family'.

Underlying the thinking of Western Asia and Europe is the notion that life is essentially a matter of opposition and conflict. We have already drawn attention to the ancient Persian addiction to contrasting opposites – good/bad, black/white, strong/weak, victory/defeat and so on. The notion of inevitable conflict has bitten deep. We are under continual pressure to choose one or the other – guilty or innocent, win or lose, right or wrong. So it is not surprising that when people in the West find themselves dissatisfied with their society they try to invent an *alternative.* If you cannot live in this society, then you must live in another. We therefore find movements of withdrawal from existing societies – out of the town into the wilderness. Flower people, hippies, 'travellers', religious sects, fringe groups and so on all opt out of existing society and try to set up a counter-society in opposition. Yet it is really not necessary to opt out or to be in opposition. Instead of an alternative society one can create a complementary society, one which modifies or makes good the excesses or deficiencies of the dominant society, to which inevitably most of the population must continue to belong. Instead of thinking in terms of sharp contrast – black or white – we need to train ourselves to be more aware of graduated shadings of grey, the scale rather than the cut. Of course in some instances stark contrast is legitimate – plus or minus, left or right, some or none – but many which until recently appeared to be clear opposites – alive or dead, male or female – are no longer found to be so. There are now for instance many different medical definitions of *dead* according to the stage reached, and sex is also graduated from male to female through various degrees of feminine-type males and masculine-type females.

A complementary society is therefore one which supplements the deficiencies of the dominant society and is able to provide relief for those who are hard pressed by it. But this is only possible if they are able to adapt their lives to a *yin-yang* rhythm. To structure one's life according to the *yin-yang* rhythm is therefore a primary objective. During the past centuries this has been almost impossible because work has been ruled by the clock and the shift system, and work has set the framework for everything else. But gradually work itself is becoming more flexible. The telephone, home computer and fax machine are setting the pace.

Western societies at present exert tremendous pressure on individuals to spend and consume far beyond their needs. This saps and rots the ethical basis of our civilisation which, in its Christian origins, is a spiritual civilisation convinced of the small importance of material things. The civilisation of the Roman Empire was thoroughly materialistic and encouraged greed for possessions. Christianity fought this for many long centuries, and though never very successful, never gave up its ideal. Today's modern societies organised for advertising encourage greed more powerfully than ever before. But, as Bruce Chatwin wrote in *The Songlines*: 'The world, if it has a future, has an ascetic future.'

REFERENCE NOTES

Chapter 7.

1. For the origin of the decimal place system and the evolution of the zero see Needham (1954), Vol.3, pp.5 ff.

2. For Wallerstein's contribution to this subject see Needham (1954), Vol.7, part 1, (forthcoming), and *Review, Fernand Braudel Center*, XV, 4, Fall 1992, p. 561 ff.

Conclusion

This book has attempted to show how for the past three centuries the world has been thrown off balance, and how Taoist ideas may help us to restore an equilibrium. Civilisation itself – the art of living in cities – is only about six thousand years old. Particular civilisations grew up wherever the soil was rich enough to permit farming with a surplus capable of supporting rulers with an army of clerks. This was usually in the river valleys where periodic flooding renewed fertility. Each civilisation thought of itself as a complete world, and was only dimly aware that others existed. Gradually each began to realise that others were comparable to their own. They would in time have come to know that each was contributing as an equal to the common store of inventions and ideas, that the world was one. But before this had come about modern science started in Western Europe and exploded.

The story of that explosion was traced at the end of Chapter 2 in the development of physics leading to nuclear fission. But similar developments were taking place simultaneously in all other fields – surgery was transformed by the discovery of anaesthetics; plant and animal breeding by the discovery of genetics; animal power gave way to the external and internal combustion engine and the use of electricity; the distance a man could hope to cover in an hour was suddenly increased a hundred fold in the air, and a thousand fold in space. The control of diseases and measures for public health sent populations rocketing, but the invention of ways of controlling reproduction made it possible to bring populations once again back to a reasonable size. Information was multiplying so rapidly that a new problem arose – assimilation, but to offset this, new inventions enormously improved the means of communication and of organising information for rapid retrieval. The arts also were caught up in the upheaval. Chemistry gave artists new and brighter colours. The mathematically equal-tempered scale transformed modal music. The period from 1600 to 2000 may be regarded as the explosive centuries. The speed at which everything has happened made adjustment to change particularly difficult.

Over us all hang clouds of misinformation, disinformation and prejudice. Modern science has so far had little effect on our patterns of thinking. We still prefer simile and analogy to cause and effect. When a new idea is lobbed into our private world we tackle it by the medieval method of disputation. New ideas are treated like prisoners in the dock, and every effort is made by partisans to establish a reputation for them, good or bad. Yet new ideas deserve to be tested fairly, in a small controlled environment, changing one variable at a time. Until recently this has been too difficult, but the means for conducting such tests and pilot projects are gradually extending and being improved. Computers now make it possible to predict results in scenarios of great complexity, and politicians will be able to introduce innovations to society with confidence. The future will belong to the first truly scientific society.

Yet science is only part of the story. It is not a guide to conduct, apart from its dedication to truth. It is not concerned with the love that passes all understanding. The real guide to conduct lies in a heightened sensitivity to the needs of others, and an awareness of our individual insignificance among the myriad things which form the process of the Tao. How this sensitivity may be heightened without recourse to the apparatus of the Bronze Age religions has been hinted at in the foregoing pages, but in greater detail will make the subject matter for another book.

Select Bibliography

Barrow, John and Silk, Joseph, *The Left Hand of Creation.* (Heinemann, London 1984. Harvester Press, 1985).

Blofeld, John. (Tr.) *The Book of Change: A new translation.* (Allen and Unwin, London 1965).

Bohm, David B. *Wholeness and the Implicate Order.* (Ark Paperbacks. Routledge Kegan and Paul, London, 1980).

Bohr, Neils. *Atomic Physics and Human Knowledge.* (John Wiley, London, 1958).

Burton, Richard. Trans. *The Perfumed Garden of the Shaykh Nefzawi,* with an introduction by Alan Hull Walton. (Book Club Associates, London, 1982, by arrangement with Neville Spearman Ltd, 1963).

Capra, Fritjof *The Tao of Physics.* (Fontana, London, 1976).

Carter, T.F. *The Invention of Printing in China and its Spread Westward.* (Columbia University Press, New York, 1925. Revised edition 1931, 2nd edition revised by L. Carrington Goodrich. Ronald, New York, 1955).

Chatwin, Bruce. *The Songlines.* (Picador. Pan Books, Cape, London, 1987).

Close, Frank, *The Cosmic Onion: Quarks and the Nature of the Universe.* (Heinemann Educational Books, London, 1983).

Davies, Paul, *Other Worlds.* (Dent, London, 1980).

God and the New Physics. (Dent, London, 1983).

Dawkins, Richard. *The Selfish Gene.* (O.U.P., Oxford, 1976).
The Blind Watchmaker. (Longmans, London, 1986).
Debiprasad Chattopadhyaya. See Mohammed Said, ed.
Douglas, Mary, *Purity and Danger: An Analysis of the Concepts of Pollution and Taboo.* (Routledge & Kegan Paul, London, 1966).
Dyson, Freeman, 'Time without End: Physics and Biology in an Open Universe', in *Review of Modern Physics,* 1979.
Eliade, Mircea, *Le Mythe de l'Eternel Retour.* (Gallimard, Paris, 1949).
Fêng Yu-Lan (Tr.) *Chuang Tzu: a new selected translation with an exposition of the philosophy of Kuo Hsiang.* (Commercial Press, Shanghai, 1933).
Giles, Lionel. *Taoist Teachings from the Book of 'Lieh Tzu'.* (Murray, London, 1912. 2nd edition, 1947, Wisdom of the East Series).
Graham, Angus C., *The Book of Lieh-tzu: A New Translation.* (Wisdom of the East series. (Murray, London, 1960).
Chuang Tzu, The Seven Inner Chapters and Other Writings from the Book Chuang Tzu. (George Allen & Unwin, London, 1981).
Gribbin, John. *The Omega Point.* (Bantam, New York; Corgi, London, 1980).
In Search of the Big Bang. (Bantam, New York; Corgi, London, 1986.
Gribbin, John and Rees, Martin, *The Stuff of the Universe, Dark Matter, Mankind and the Coincidences of Cosmology.* (Heinemann, London, 1990).
Hawking, Stephen. *A Brief History of Time: From the Big Bang to Black Holes.* Introduction by Carl Sagan. (Space Time Publications, Guild Publishing, London, 1988).
(Ed.) *A Brief History of Time: A Reader's Companion.* Prepared by Gene Stone. (Bantam Press. London, 1992).

Heisenberg, Werner, *Physics and Philosophy.* (Allen and Unwin, London, 1959).

Hemming, James. *Instead of God. A Pragmatic Reconsideration of Beliefs and Values.* (Marion Boyars Publishers Ltd, London and New York, 1986).

Huang Su-Shu, 'Physics of Life' in the *Ta-You Wu Festschrift; Science of Matter,* pp. 253-272. (Gordon & Breach, New York, 1978).

Idries Shah, *The Sufis.* Introduction by Robert Graves. (Jonathan Cape, paperback, London, 1969. First published W. H. Allen & Co., London, 1964).

Karlgren, B. (Tr.) *The Book of Odes: Chinese Text, Transcription and Translation.* (Museum of Far Eastern Antiquities, Stockholm, 1950).

Koyré, Alexandre, *From the Closed World to the Infinite Universe.* (John Hopkins Press, Baltimore, 1957).

Ladurie, Emmanuel Leroy, *Montaillou.* 1978. (Penguin Books, London, 1980).

Lau, D.C., (Trans.) *Tao Te Ching.* (Chinese University Press, Hong Kong, 1982).

Legge, James. (Tr.) The Chinese Classics, etc.: Vol. 1. *Confucian Analects, The Great Learning, and the Doctrine of the Mean.* (Legge, Hongkong. 1861. Trübner, London, 1861).

(Tr.) The Chinese Classics, etc.: Vol. 4, Parts I and II. *The Book of Poetry.* (Lane Crawford, Hongkong, 1871. Trübner, London, 1871).

(Tr.) The Texts of Confucianism, Part II. *The 'Yi King'* [*I Ching*], (Oxford, 1882).

(Tr.) The Texts of Confucianism, Part III, *The Li Chi.* 2 vols. (Oxford, 1885).

(Tr.) *The Texts of Taoism.* 2 vols. (Oxford, 1891).

Millard, Alan, *Discoveries from the Time of Jesus.* (Lion Publishing; Oxford, 1990).

Mohammed Said, Hakim., Ed. *Essays on Science, Felicitation Volume in Honour of Dr Joseph Needham.* (Hamdard Foundation Pakistan, Karachi, 1990).

Needham, Joseph. *The Great Amphibium.* (Student Christian Movement Press, London, 1931).

Science and Civilisation in China, seven volumes, some multipart. (Cambridge University Press, 1954 ongoing).

Ne'eman, Yuval & Kirsh, Yoram, *The Particle Hunters,* (up-dated version). (C.U.P. Cambridge, 1986. English translation of *Tsayade ha-helkikim.* Original Hebrew version by Massada, Israel, 1983).

Nefzawi, Shaykh. See Burton.

Pagels, Elaine. *The Gnostic Gospels.* Wiedenfeld and Nicolson, London, 1980.

Pagels, Heinz, *The Cosmic Code: Quantum Physics as the Language of Nature.* (Michael Joseph, 1983).

Polkinghorne, J.C, *The Quantum World.* (Penguin Books, Harmondsworth, 1986. First pub. Longman, 1984).

Popper, Karl, *The Open Society and its Enemies.* (Routledge, London, 1945 and Longmans, London, 1984).

Sagan, Carl, *Cosmos* (Random House, New York, 1980).

Singleton, W.T., *The Mind at Work, Psychological Ergonomics.* (C.U.P., Cambridge, 1989).

Vickers, D, *Decision Processes in Visual Perception.* (Academic Press, London, 1979).

Waley, Arthur. *The Way and its Power. A Study of the Tao Tê Ching and Its Place in Chinese Thought.* (Allen & Unwin, London, 1934).

The Book of Songs. (Allen & Unwin, London, 1937).

The Analects of Confucius. (Allen and Unwin, London, 1938).

Three Ways of Thought in Ancient China. (Allen & Unwin, London, 1939).

Wells, H.G., *The Wheels of Chance* and *The Time Machine.* (Everyman's Library No. 915 Dent, London, 1935. First published 1895).

Wilson, A.N., *Jesus.* (Sinclair-Stevenson, London, 1992).

Chinese Book List

The following works are cited or referred to in the preceding chapters.

Chuang Tzu, 'The Book of Master Chuang'. Written by Chuang Chou, the Taoist philosopher, in about 290 BC. A teasing, lyrical and provocative book, first translated into English by James Legge in 1891, and susequently by others in whole or in part. See Fêng Yu-Lan, 1933. Angus C. Graham, 1981.

Hou Han Shu, 'The History of the Later Han Dynasty,' by Fan Yeh, AD 450. The Later Han Dynasty lasted from AD 25 to 220, being roughly contemporary with the Roman Empire, whereas the Former Han Dynasty (206 BC to AD 24) was roughly contemporary with the great days of the Roman Republic. No complete English translation.

Huai Nan Tzu, 'The Book of (the Prince of) Huai Nan'. A compendium of natural philosophy written about 120 BC by a group of scholars brought together by the Prince of Huai Nan of the Former Han Dynasty, whose name was given to the work. No complete English translation.

Huang Chi Ching Shih Shu, 'The Book of the Sublime Principle which Governs all Things within the World', written by the Taoist philosopher Shao Yung about AD 1060. It aims to give a rational account based on number of the evolution of everything in the world, and contains the *Kuan Wu P'ien.* 'Treatise on the Observation of Things.' Very little of the work has been translated into any language.

I Ching, 'The Book of Change' (or 'The Classic of Changes'). Originally this was a fortune-teller's handbook dating from the middle of the first millenium BC. Of folk origin, its compilers are unknown, but it was later refined by sophisticated thinkers, which, with its undoubted antiquity, gave it an authority for which there is little scientific justification. Translated by James Legge in 1882, John Blofeld in 1965.

Kuan Tzu, 'The Book of Master Kuan'. This ancient work on natural philosophy and economics was compiled towards the end of the fourth century BC perhaps mainly by scholars of the famous Chi Hsia Academy. It included earlier materials justifying its attribution to Kuan Chung, a Minister of the State of Ch'i, who had lived three hundred years before. No complete English translation.

Lieh Tzu, 'The Book of Master Lieh'. This book was not compiled till about AD 380, but contains much material dating from the fifth to the third centuries BC. It is a most entertaining book putting forward Taoist ideas, and has been translated by Lionel Giles in 1912 and Angus C. Graham in 1966.

Lun Yü, 'Conversations and Discourses (of Confucius)'. The sayings of Confucius were committed to writing in this great classic of China in about the year 460 BC, that is to say, about ten years after the birth of Socrates. Rigorously avoiding speculating about the supernatural, Confucius nevertheless bequeathed to his disciples a memory and example resulting in what may not unreasonably be described as a 'Testament of Social Conduct'. Translated by James Legge in 1861, and many others thereafter. See especially Waley, 1938.

Pao P'u Tzu, 'The Book of the Master who is able to Preserve Solidarity', by Ko Hung, the great Taoist alchemist of the fourth century AD. His 'Outer Chapters' deal with social and political matters, and the 'Inner Chapters' with alchemical questions. No complete translations.

Shih Ching, 'The Classic of Ancient Songs' was compiled between the ninth and the fifth centuries BC. What had been originally a collection of folk songs, many of great antiquity even in Confucius' day, were later given sophisticated or courtly interpretations, and used to point a moral. Translated by Legge in 1871, Waley in 1937, and Karlgren in 1950.

Tao Tê Ching, 'The Classic of the Way and of Power'. This inspiring work, much of it of sublime poetry, was originally two books, 'The Classic of the Way', and 'The Classic of [Moral] Power', but was later shortened and edited to a single volume. The author is unknown but evidently lived in about 300 BC. It was attributed to a semi-legendary philosopher Lao Tzu. There are many translations, the earliest in English by Legge, 1891. Waley, 1934, still provides here an excellent and readable introduction to Taoist thought. D.C. Lau's translation (1982) has the advantage of recently discovered earlier versions of the manuscript.

Yüeh Ling, 'The Monthly Ordinances (of the Chou Dynasty)'. The 'Son of Heaven', and later the emperors of China, were held to be the vital conductors of cosmic forces bringing well-being or disaster to their people. The affairs of the court therefore had to be conducted with the strictest propriety if disasters were to be avoided. This meant that every action should be in conformity with the Tao, the Way of Nature, even in such small matters as wearing clothing of a colour conforming to the season. Beginning with court rules in the seventh century BC it ended as a detailed and sophisticated compilation in the third century BC which, if carefully followed, would, it was hoped, ensure stability in human affairs. Translated by Legge in 1885.

Index